FEMINIST READINGS / SERIES EDITOR: SUE ROE

James Joyce

FEMINIST READINGS / SERIES EDITOR: SUE ROE

James Joyce

BONNIE KIME SCOTT

Professor of English
University of Delaware

HUMANITIES PRESS INTERNATIONAL, INC.

Atlantic Highlands, NJ

First published in 1987 in the United States of America by
HUMANITIES PRESS INTERNATIONAL, INC.,
Atlantic Highlands, NJ 07716

© Bonnie Kime Scott, 1987

Library of Congress Cataloging-in-Publication Data

Scott, Bonnie Kime, 1944–
   James Joyce.
   (Feminist readings)
   Bibliography: p.
   Includes index.
   1. Joyce, James 1822–1941—Characters—Women.
2. Women in literature. 3. Feminism and literature.
I. Title. II. Series.
PR6019.09Z79444   1987   823'.912   87–3701
ISBN 0–391–03524–X
ISBN 0–391–03525–8 (pbk.)

PRINTED IN GREAT BRITAIN

To my mother
Sheila Burton Kime

Feminist Readings

Series Editor: Sue Roe

The *Feminist Readings* series has been designed to investigate the link between literary writing and feminist reading by surveying the key works of English Literature by male authors from new feminist perspectives.

Working from a position which accepts that the notion of gender difference embraces interrelationship and reciprocity as well as opposition, each contributor to the series takes on the challenge of reassessing the problems inherent in confronting a 'phallocentric' literary canon, by investigating the processes involved in the translation of gender difference into the themes and structures of the literary text.

Each volume surveys briefly the development of feminist literary criticism and the broader questions of feminism which have been brought to bear on this practice, from the initial identification of 'phallocentrism', through the tendency of early feminist critics to read literature as a sociological document, through to feminist criticism's current capacity to realign the discoveries of a wide range of disciplines in order to reassess theories of gender difference. The tendency of the feminist critic to privilege texts written by women and the notion that it might be possible to identify an autonomous tradition of 'women's writing' can offer a range of challenges to current feminist criticism, and the key texts by male authors surveyed by the series are considered in this light.

Can there be a politics of feminist criticism? How might a theory of sexual difference be seen to be directly applicable to critical practice? The series as a whole represents a comprehensive survey of the development of various theories of gender difference, and, by assessing their applicability to the writing of the most influential male writers of the literary tradition, offers a broadly revisionary interpretation of feminist critical practice.

Louise DeSalvo	*Nathaniel Hawthorne*
Bonnie Kime Scott	*James Joyce*
Julia Briggs	*Shakespeare*
Jacqueline Di Salvo	*Milton*
Sandra Gilbert	*T.S. Eliot*
Patricia Ingham	*Thomas Hardy*
Kate McLuskie	*Renaissance Dramatists*
Jill Mann	*Geoffrey Chaucer*
Marion Shaw	*Alfred Lord Tennyson*
Margarita Stocker	*Marvell*

Contents

Abbreviations

Joyce's texts are all referred to parenthetically. Abbreviations are used for any references to his works that are not obvious in the immediate context. Citations to the 1984 edition of *Ulysses* state chapter and line numbers, not page number, a system suggested by its editors. This text was chosen because from 1986 onward, it became the basis of the Penguin student edition in Europe and the Random House edition in the US. For *Finnegans Wake*, page and line numbers are provided, as is customary.

CP   Joyce, James. *Collected Poems*. New York: Viking Press, 1957.

CW   Joyce, James. *The Critical Writings of James Joyce*, ed Ellsworth Mason and Richard Ellmann. New York: Viking Press, 1959.

D   Joyce, James. *'Dubliners': Text, Criticism, and Notes*, ed Robert Scholes and A. Walton Litz. New York: Viking Press, 1969.

E   Joyce, James. *Exiles*. New York: Viking Press, 1951.

FW   Joyce, James. *Finnegans Wake*. New York: Viking Press, 1939.

J&F   Scott, Bonnie. *Joyce and Feminism*. Bloomington: Indiana University Press and Sussex: Harvester Press, 1984.

JJ   Ellmann, Richard. *James Joyce*, new and revised ed. New York and Oxford: Oxford University Press, 1982.

L   Joyce, James. *Letters of James Joyce*. Vol. I, ed Stuart Gilbert. New York: Viking Press, 1965. Vols. II and III, ed Richard Ellmann. New York: Viking Press, 1966.

P   Joyce, James. *'A Portrait of the Artist as a Young Man': Text, Criticism, and Notes*, ed Chester G. Anderson. New York: Viking Press, 1968.

SH   Joyce, James. *Stephen Hero*, ed John J. Slocum and Herbert Cahoon. New York: New Directions, 1963.

SL   Joyce, James. *Selected Letters of James Joyce*, ed Richard Ellmann. New York: Viking Press, 1975.

U   Joyce, James. *'Ulysses': A Critical and Synoptic Edition*, ed Hans Walter Gabler. New York and London: Garland Publishing, Inc., 1984.

Preface and Acknowledgements

While many of the works in the Harvester Feminist Readings series constitute the first book-length feminist reading of a male author, this is not only a second feminist volume on Joyce, but *my* second one. In *Joyce and Feminism* (1984) I presented feminist historical and biographical backgrounds for Joyce and began my feminist reading of his texts with studies of three women characters who appear in different major novels. Readers of this book may want to refer directly to these basic materials. Since I see my work as connected and ongoing, let me summarize my handling of the three Joycean women selected for *Joyce and Feminism,* so that they may join additional ones presented in this volume. In *Stephen Hero,* Joyce's early version of *A Portrait of the Artist as a Young Man,* Emma Clery plays opposite Stephen Dedalus, whose perceptions of her include muse and goddess. But Emma has a set of aspirations that had been neglected in previous criticism. I have examined her educational and nationalist interests as aspects of female culture in Joyce's background. Molly Bloom, Joyce's most written-about woman and the final voice in *Ulysses,* emerged in my study with several roles. As a realistic character she takes on the values and limitations of identities such as Jew, child of the Gibraltar garrison, and Dubliner—in the aspects of married woman, mother and female artiste. More forcefully, she also plays an iconoclast whose complaints coincide with much of the feminist consciousness-raising of her own era and of the late 1960s. Finally, I questioned the ideologies behind usual critical interpretations of her as earth mother and offered new goddess associations, particularly from the Celtic world. Mythic dimensions of Molly's character are pursued further in chapter 4 of this book. The third female character of *Joyce and Feminism* was Issy, the daughter figure of *Finnegans Wake,* and like Emma Clery, a young woman with intellectual potential. Issy uses wit, sarcasm and linguistic invention to comment upon patriarchal culture and to respond to the artist figure of the *Wake.* She also has mythical dimensions—including identifications with the Egyptian goddess, Isis, and Deirdre, a fugitive from patriarchal plot in Irish myth. These studies only began feminist character analysis in Joyce.

The present book offers additional analyses of Joycean women, particularly ones that have been called for by readers of *Joyce and Feminism:* Gretta Conroy of the story, 'The Dead', from *Dubliners,* Bertha Rowan and Beatrice Justice from the play *Exiles,* Gerty MacDowell of *Ulysses,* and ALP, the mother figure of *Finnegans Wake.* I have extended feminist analysis to male characters, particularly Stephen and Simon Dedalus, in *A Portrait* and *Ulysses.*

But I am no longer content with character analysis as a representation of feminist theoretical options, or as an approach to Joyce, who broke down traditional concepts of character in *Ulysses* and *Finnegans Wake.* Each of chapters 2-5 takes up an issue currently under feminist debate, directing the tools and questions presented toward selected Joyce texts. I call upon, not just one feminist approach, but the variety that is needed to deal both with the issues under discussion, and Joyce's writing. It would be impossible in a book of this scope to represent the full variety and complex history of feminist theories. But to make the theories I deal with clear conceptually, I have arranged them in a 'matrix of feminist theory'. As explained in chapter 1, this is appropriate to the 'plurabilities' (*FW* 104.2) of both Joyce and contemporary feminism. The matrix can be used to overlay the human territories (conscious and unconscious, realistic and fantastic, individual and collective) explored by Joyce. By treating such conceptual differences, it clarifies the grounds of disagreements among seemingly rival feminist practices and the interests specific feminist practices share with non-feminist theory.

Some readers may object that a critic cannot simply wander in and out of radical Marxist, post-structuralist or lesbian critical practices, that one must ardently believe in one feminist approach or another. My matrix method probably disqualifies this work as radical, unless its whole questioning of monological thinking be accepted as such. Its pluralism exists, not for placation and survival, but for comprehension, in both its cognitive and inclusive senses. This is an ideological position that resists a singular, linear, codified approach or polemic in favour of an awareness of how theory or literature must be focused upon diversely, multidimensionally, and in juxtaposition to alternate sets of practices in order to yield its full implications. On the other hand, the critical plurabilities presented here prepare readers to apply distinct feminist practices more concertedly, having seen the sorts of Joycean textual situations where they work well.

Among my readers, I expect to find some who are cognizant of and even involved in the development of feminist theory, and some interested and experienced in Joyce's texts. Especially at the start of this work, I must occasionally ask for patience from one of these sets of readers while treating the needs or interests of the other. It is likely that a great number of my readers will be students who are not familiar with Joyce or feminist theory, and I hope to excite them in both areas, without presenting a theoretical overload. Theoretical terms are defined as they appear. The terms and issues introduced in chapter 1 become the tools for the Joycean textual explorations in the four topics that follow.

For the purposes of this book, I should like to define and document myself as a Joycean feminist (in other contexts and projects, I would not do so). I was already involved in the study of Joyce before the current era of feminist criticism began, and long before it reached me. But in my first sustained critical writing—an undergraduate honours thesis—I studied Joyce alongside Virginia Woolf. I was a Joycean pre-feminist, sometimes seeing Joyce through Woolf, instead of the other way around. I identified with the struggles of a feminist reader, Julia Hedge, in Woolf's *Jacob's Room*, who asked questions not easily researched in the libraries of her day, adorned, as they were, with male names.[1] A Woolfian-Joycean method survives, with recent feminist theoretical support, in the present work. I do not believe that I am still studying Joyce because of a long-term investment in him, or because of the cultural urge of the daughter to do homage to father figures and great men of literature. In my opinion, Joyce's works merit feminist attention primarily because they give considerable dimension and variety to the investigation of gender in language and life, and we gain a new sense of Joyce and modernism by taking up the issues selected for this study.

The feminist side of my designation began, predictably, with an Anglo-American tendency—an orientation to be explained more thoroughly in chapter 1. My first interests were to recover the real women around Joyce, and to investigate the role of women Joyce selected to depict as characters. Also predictably, two of the three women I selected were comparable to myself, as women with intellectual aspirations. Like Joyce, I subsequently found the Continent a valuable wandering ground. In my case, this has meant an attraction to French feminist theory. The discovery was inevitable to a Joycean of my generation. Keeping up with Joyce studies in the last decade has required acquaintance with French psychoanalytic and linguistic approaches to Joyce. Joycean feminists—and there are a growing number both in Europe and America—have tended to be more comfortable with and interested in Continental theory than most American feminists, and have done their own adapting of it to feminist concerns. Out of this sort of experience, an American Joycean feminist may be able to provide a valuable overview of current feminist practices, while setting them to work on Joyce.

This book has been greatly assisted by colleagues willing to share their own work in progress. I want to thank Shari Benstock, Penny Boumhela, Sandra Gilbert, Elliott Gose, Karen Lawrence, Toril Moi and Richard Pearce for such trusting and constructive exchanges. The Oxford Women's Studies Committee welcomed me to their sessions in spring 1984, which assisted me in diversifying my sense of feminist theory. Discussions arising from the formation of the Women's Caucus of the James Joyce Foundation and its subsequent informal sessions have offered me a sense of direction in placing Joyce within a revisionary modernist project. My students have helped me find my way in Joyce's texts and have tested out the theoretical groundings offered in this work. I thank Suzette Henke, Zack Bowen, Patrick Parrinder, Ruth Bauerle, Elliott Gose, and Phil Goldstein for valuable reactions to all or part of the manuscript. Series editor, Sue Roe, has been a source of encouragement throughout the composition process. My children, Heather, Ethan and Heidi, are to be complimented for giving me uninterrupted time before a home-based word processor. I am grateful to my husband, Tom Scott, for the blend of toleration, interest and support that are essential to the flourishing of a marriage, particularly one between over-working academics.

I should like to gratefully acknowledge permission to reprint passages from *A Portrait of the Artist as a Young Man* by Viking Penguin Inc. and the Society of Authors; from *Ulysses* by the Society of Authors; and from *Finnegans Wake* by Viking Penguin Inc. and the Society of Authors.

CHAPTER ONE

Plurabilities: Joyce in a Matrix of Feminist Theory

Few writers invite such quantity and diversity of critical study as James Joyce. There are several explanations for this. He takes up problems that we still probe in this postmodern age: effects of urbanization, technology, and capitalism; movement away from traditional western literature and philosophy; the emergence of diverse popular media; the politics of colonialism, race, class structure, and relations between the sexes; and exploration of the unconscious, including its relationships to language, gender, and sexual models. He writes in diverse forms that invite varied critical approaches, as well as a varied readership: formal essays and book reviews, delicate lyrics, realistic or naturalistic short stories, a problem play and finally, part way into *Ulysses* and throughout *Finnegans Wake,* constant shifts of style that break down formal and cultural assumptions and may result in the deconstruction (undermining of a supposed system of meaning) of language itself.

As we shall discover, the study of Joyce conflicts with some forms of feminist ideology. Feminist separatists might ask, 'Why take up a male author when there are so many neglected women writers?' Joyce has become the central star in a constellation of great male modernists, a literary movement largely defined by men such as Ezra Pound, T.S. Eliot, Wyndham Lewis, and their male successors in academe. Joyce's difficulty and the remote critical discourses that have responded to it are offputting to advocates of an accessible, egalitarian feminism. Joyce studies have had their share of sexual politics. The Joycean critical canon has been superintended by men, and male critics have emerged as its stars and its privileged theoreticians, though women began to occupy more visible positions in the late 1970s.[1] This chapter includes a sober assessment of the political perils of working with Joyce in feminist terms, in addition to its inviting possibilites.

To my mind, there are several requirements for criticism to be designated 'feminist'. It is not necessary or sufficient that the critic be female, that s/he write about female characters or about women writers, or that s/he adopt a feminist identification. I include here as feminists some who would not embrace the title.[2] The 'ist' part of feminist suggests ideological alliance to the women's movement as it re-emerged in the late 1960s, alongside the civil rights movement, the peace movement, and the upheavals in the French universities. Today's feminist literary theories owe a great deal to precursors of the 1920s—expecially Virginia Woolf. Feminists challenge cultural hegemony (established practices, acquiesced to by the masses), attending to various questions and definitions of gender difference. These include questioning male dominance of the literary and critical canons (texts viewed as culturally central, standard works to be read and taught), exposing the limitations of various behaviours and discourses expected in patriarchal society, and replacing male-centred psychoanalytical, linguistic, and mythical paradigms (models). Instead of seeing literature as pure and disinterested, feminist critics are apt to detect previously unassessed power structures (politics) in the text and in its production. They aspire to creative, renovating critical practices, and eagerly question their own.

In the four chapters that follow, we will be taking up some of the principal issues and positions entertained in contemporary feminist theories. The next chapter (chapter 2) investigates Joyce's representation of and challenges to canonized literature and male-dominated history. Chapter 3 studies gender in a social setting, more specifically the discourses of men and women of Dublin, as rendered in selections from Joyce's early writing. Chapter 4 turns to more abstract, imaginative forms, assessing Joyce's rewritings of classical and psychoanalytic myths, in comparison to feminist reconstructions of these materials. Chapter 5 takes up the controversial possibility of feminine language, searching out Joyce's attempts in his later, most experimental writing. Chapters 2 and 3 focus on the representational, realistic rendering of the conscious world; chapters 4 and 5 are more concerned with unconscious realms expressed in fantastic and imaginative forms.

As suggested in the preface, no single feminist approach represents the complexity of these four subjects. Nor would a single approach be able to follow Joyce's own development. To express it very simply (and there are exceptions), the young Joyce was largely a realistic, individualistic, logocentric (word-centred) writer who subscribed to a classical aesthetic of stasis. The mature Joyce became a collectivist, a deconstructionist, and a mythologist of the unconscious. I am therefore offering a matrix of selected contemporary feminist theory relevant to the central issues of each chapter and the Joycean texts they feature. In the vertical dimension, the matrix moves through similar conceptual focuses to the ones that Joyce took up in the course of his writing, ranging from realistic, historical concepts (at the top) through imaginary paradigms for the unconscious (at the bottom). In a long box to the right of the matrix is a list of Joyce's works used in this book which aligns them with this vertical or conceptual range. In its left-right dimension, the matrix charts the attitude of specific feminist practices toward male-related projects. As already noted, a critical issue in feminist debates today, and one inescapable in taking up Joyce, is whether feminists should separate themselves from male-produced literary texts and theory.

The feminist matrix locates practices in overlapped male+ feminist territory (left) and separate female territory (right), an area where male critics rarely venture. Female critics have long read a fairly exclusive male zone of criticism, and

A MATRIX OF CONTEMPORARY FEMINIST CRITICAL PRACTICES

←Horizontal range—orientation to separatism→

Overlapped feminist-male theory and writing → *Separate female theory and writing*

←Vertical range—conceptual orientation→

Representational

FEMINIST SOCIALISTS AND MARXISTS 1920s–1980s (UK, US)

Collective Conscious

MAINSTREAMING 1980 (US)

GYNOCRITICISM 1975 (US, some UK)

Lesbian feminists 1970s (US, France)

Personal Conscious

Consciousness raisers early 1970s (US, France)
Feminist reader response 1979

ÉCRITURE FÉMININE 1980 (France)

Personal Unconscious

FEMINIST POST-STRUCTURALISM 1974 (France, some UK)

Collective Unconscious

FEMINIST MYTH 1920s on (diverse cultures)

Imaginative

JOYCE'S WORKS

- first half *Ulysses*
- *Dubliners*
- *Exiles*
- *A Portrait*
- second half *Ulysses*
- *Finnegans Wake*

their knowledge of it and of the shared zone, may assist their critical revolution. One complaint of feminists is that male critics, including the fashionable deconstructionists, have not recognized their debts to new feminist work in their overlapped field; this seems a liability of the politics of feminist overlap,[3] and a pattern feminists working with Joyce should be wary of.

The Marxist, socialist and feminist post-structuralist practices situated toward the left of the matrix consider male as well as female writers; they are integrated to some degree in the newer theoretical areas of the male-dominated critical community, and accept the theoretical paradigms proposed by celebrated men. Though dismissed or pursued as stylish, these theorists regard themselves as marginal in relation to traditional male critical theory.[4] Many traditional Joyceans continue to question the merits of recent theory, as has been evident in discussion periods at recent Joyce conferences.[5] This can put Joycean feminists in a double bind—suspect as marginals by the conservative group, and still marginal to other advanced theorists.

Feminist practices situated toward the right of the matrix concentrate on female writers and female social and psychological experiences. They search for a muted culture, common but trivialized women's experiences, neglected myths, texts and genres, repressed psychological, sexual and linguistic traits. The term 'gynocritic', proposed by Elaine Showalter, is broadly applicable to this position, as it calls for 'sustained investigations of literature by women', and seeks to define a tradition of women's literature.[6] My situation of *écriture féminine* to the right is somewhat debatable, depending on how rigorously biological sex is used as a stylistic model—a point we return to. Between integrated and separatist feminist positions are approaches that challenge men's writing, theory, and representations of cultural history. Work in this position began with the practical endeavour of consciousness-raising. Isolated awakenings to the stereotypes and power structures of male hegemony came from critics like Simone de Beauvoir, Mary Ellmann and Kate Millett. A recent development in this part of the field is feminist reader response theory. I shall return to mainstreaming, another practice in the middle area.

The lines that divide top and bottom, right and left of the matrix are permeable, and theoretical positions may shift. Catherine MacKinnon argues that consciousness-raising remains a central method of feminist criticism. Showalter sees a shift toward her own ground of gynocriticism.[7] The prominence of gynocriticism is challenged by projects like this feminist readings series and other recent feminist studies of male authors like William Shakespeare, D.H. Lawrence and Thomas Hardy. An admirable, growing tradition of feminist criticism on Joyce now exists.[8] Though French post-structuralists have begun to write on women, they are far from relinquishing their male subjects. In *Sexual/Textual Politics,* Toril Moi calls attention to what she considers unexamined ideological limitations of gynocriticism, including its realist orientation; she directs her readers to French feminist post-structuralism (theory occupied with the mechanisms of textuality as related to a writing and reading psychoanalytical subject).[9] I think that for its full effect on culture, feminist criticism must engage with male writers resourcefully and with a thorough knowledge of their texts.

A new centrally-situated endeavour is 'mainstreaming' or 'rebalancing the curriculum', which brings the lessons of separate women's studies and the research on other muted or marginal groups like blacks and colonials to bear on the canon. The goal is to change what is read and taught, how it is conceptualized, and how it is communicated, rejecting many received notions of cultural and academic authority.[10] As we shall see in chapter 2, these types of challenge are quite relevant to Joyce, who entered a new curriculum of modern literature in his own day, having encountered a classical canon in his early Jesuit education. His work refers to an older canon, but reacts, challenges and replaces it as well. Joyce's canonical status is at stake, if canonization is to survive, and we may not wish it to.

To fulfill its goal of comprehending Joyce, this study selects feminist approaches that are widely distributed in the matrix. These include: feminist socialism and Marxism (upper left), mainstreaming (upper centre), gynocriticism (upper right), post-structuralist feminism (lower left), feminist myth (lower centre) and *écriture féminine* (lower right), and are printed in capitals for easy spotting on the matrix. When realists study Joyce, they are drawn first to *Dubliners,* but also find much to work with in *A Portrait of the Artist as a Young Man,* in *Exiles* and in the less experimental early chapters of *Ulysses.* These become the texts concentrated upon in chapter 2, on canonized literature and history, and in chapter 3, on gender in social discourses. Appropriately, the feminist approaches featured in these chapters come from the top of the vertical or conceptual orientation of the matrix. Irish cultural separation of the sexes is a factor in both of these chapters, so the horizontal or separatist orientation of the matrix remains of interest. When psychoanalysts, linguists and mythologists study Joyce, they find valuable materials in the earlier texts. But their favoured texts are the more fantastic, dreamlike, linguistically inventive later chapters of *Ulysses* and all of *Finnegans Wake.* These are the texts that dominate chapter 4, on myth, and chapter 5, on language. While separate male experience may seem to dominate chapters 2 and 3, the emphasis on the feminine in myth and language establishes a gender balance in the book as a whole.

Once we perceive the conceptual orientations of distinct feminist positions, we can understand much of the argument that has taken place among feminist theorists of different persuasions, relate these to the general problems of feminist analysis of Joyce, and make wise choices of feminist tools for specific Joyce texts.

Gynocritics have cultivated feminist criticism in the largely separate interdisciplinary domain of women's studies; in the US, few universities lack such a programme. Showalter's separatism shows, not just in her concentration on women writers, but also in her suspicion of male-initiated contemporary theoretical practices. Rather than consult with the conspicuous men of post-structuralism (Geoffrey Hartman, Pierre Macherey, Jacques Derrida, etc.), Showalter prefers to take concepts from feminists in other disciplines. She is wary of the scientific aspects of the literary discourses 'imported from the continent', their supposed 'rigor' offering a 'virility' that fails to appeal to the female critic. Some years ago, Showalter refused to consider post-structuralist Julia Kristeva a feminist because of Kristeva's suggestion that women should not stand on the sidelines of post-structuralist criticism. To Showalter, this showed a lack of sisterly empathy to women's 'exclusion' and even 'purging' from a male domain. Showalter has moderated this attitude over the years, and her essays have shown increasing familiarity with French theory, though not perhaps with its own inward divisions (marked on our matrix by the two categories, 'post-structuralist' and *écriture féminine*).[11] She continues to remind us, however, of the risks taken by early gynocritics and to feature women's work on women.[12] Sandra Gilbert and Susan Gubar mount a witty assault on the fashionable French 'Derridaughters': 'One cannot help wondering if one is encountering a kind of intellectual *haute couture,* an Yves St Laurent of the mind which glows with glamour when set against the dowdiness of America's "garment district" empiricism'. They reassert the value of an experiential perspective and their scepticism about the adequacy of Derrida and psychoanalyst Jacques Lacan as foundations for feminism.

The gynocritic's sense of alienation from the post-structuralist avant-garde must concern the Joycean feminist, who is involved with a writer of an avant-garde tradition and one who has been much attended to by post-structuralists. While Showalter, Gilbert and Gubar have worked very successfully with nineteenth-century writers, they seem to experience incompatibility with the imaginative gambits of modernist experimentation. Showalter's negative assessment of the aesthetics of Virginia Woolf may betray her own lack of affinity with linguistic and symbolic gestures of deconstruction.[13] Gilbert and Gubar seem willing to make Joyce a target in their research into female modernism; they suggest that his attractiveness to post-structuralists is a form of guilt by association.[14] Though they condemn Derridean feminists for using a male critical language, gynocritics employ methods and frameworks used by an earlier generation of male critics. They centre on individual authors, collect historical and textual data empirically, and perform close analysis of images in texts, as did the historical and new critics of the 1950s. These techniques, coupled to feminist questions, do serve Joyce, especially in his most realistic texts, but are not sufficient to the later ones and to the critical problem of gender in language. This limitation was pointed out by European feminists to a predominately American, character-oriented feminist panel at the 1982 Joyce symposium.

Still, thanks to Anglo-American gynocriticism, the Joycean feminist sees Joyce in a different literary context, with neglected modern women authors added, and has a sense that we may have known in the past mainly a masculine version of modernism. Some of the aspects of women's culture that they have identified will prove useful in our examination of feminine discourse in chapter 3 and in our study of feminine language in chapter 5. This includes experiences related to sexuality, such as childbirth and menstruation. Of special interest are socially-inspired nurturing acts like gardening, feeding and healing, as well as dominated conditions of subordination, marginality, and interruptability. Annette Kolodny draws our attention to systems of signs decipherable only by those who are familiar with female cultural territories and willing to consider them important.[15] The emerging patterns of 'female modernism' give us new criteria for judging Joyce and for comparing him to other male modernists. How does his deconstruction of cultural norms for men and women, or of fictional narrative, his feminine language and his rewriting of myth compare with Woolf, H.D. or Stein? With Eliot, Pound, Lewis or Lawrence?

Probably the most radical rejection of male-inspired theory has come from lesbian feminists and practitioners of *écriture féminine*. Monique Wittig refuses the definition of woman that functions in heterosexual, patriarchal society.

Susan Griffin expresses suspicion of 'methodolatry'. Her
critical work has its own rules of composition—a searching,
questioning, listing, associational, allusive, highly personal
and physical discourse.[16] One representative of *écriture
féminine,* Luce Irigaray, calls for a deliberate movement
away from the cultural forms inaugurated by the Greeks—
'logic, the prevalence of the gaze, discrimination of form,
and individualization of form', finding these 'particularly
foreign to female eroticism'.[17] They were, of course, starting points for Joyce's aesthetics, and are an issue in chapters
2 and 4, which both take up Joyce's experience of classical
models.

The prose forms of *écriture féminine* and some lesbian
feminism have as their resource the psychologically repressed female.[18] Like non-feminist post-structuralism,
they share a focus on the unconscious, yet shift theory
toward a female norm and form. I assign French feminist
Hélène Cixous partially to the separatist *écriture féminine*
practice of feminism, and partly to feminist mythology.
Describing the stage when she wrote her thesis on James
Joyce, she says, 'I invested very little in the academic type
of production'. She found it 'very constraining' and admits
'I don't have good memories of it'.[19] Cixous uses her own
dreams for access to woman's 'desire', and suggests that
women have special access to the feminine, though men like
Joyce have approached it. She finds 'male' myths of acquisition and castration irrelevant to the female unconscious,
the starting place for feminine writing. She gives voice
instead to the mother who has archaic authority. The open,
moving, tactile forms Cixous cultivates in her writing have
analogies in female biology. A 'feminine textual body',
summarized as female libidinal economy, also has social
aspects of giving, dispersing, laughter, and rejection of
acquisitional goals. It escapes limitations of family and
ego.[20] Cixous' description of the feminine text as endless,
wandering, circulating from body to body, immediately
suggests the functions of Joyce's Anna Livia Plurabelle
(ALP), an identification we will develop in chapter 5.
Perhaps Joyce writes the feminine. Perhaps his textualiz-

ation of the female body in the latter part of *Ulysses* and in the *Wake* also makes it difficult for contemporary practitioners of *écriture féminine* to see their own subject immediately and clearly.

Feminists who work on texts by men as well as ones by women are less content with a biologically determined gender distinction or method of selecting whom to study. For them the 'feminine' identification is not inborn and need not be limited to biologically female subjects. Feminist revisions of the Jungian models of the 'anima' in the male and 'animus' in the female, and some concepts of androgyny support this liberation from biological determinism.

Feminist practices which have overlapped male theory offer justifications for the Joycean feminist's handling of a male author's texts. They attempt to appropriate men's literary and theoretical texts without being subject to their unexamined biases or serving as a 'ladies auxiliary of the male critical community'.[21] The Marxist-Feminist Literary Collective, for example, prefaces a discussion of nineteenth-century women writers with comments upon the limitations of Georg Lukacs and Friedrich Engels, but appropriates Lacan's psychoanalytic linguistics and Macherey's Marxism 'to analyze incoherence and contradictions in texts'. They ally this to a feminist awareness of 'the marginal position of female literary practice' during the period of industrial capitalism of the 1840s.[22]

Resistance to Freudian psychoanalysis began from within in the 1920s, with Karen Horney, Karl Abraham, Ernest Jones and Melanie Klein, who offered alternate paradigms for such controversial and blatantly male-centred concepts as the Oedipus Complex, the castration complex and the female child's 'penis envy'.[23] But what of Jacques Lacan, who has created divisions among French feminists, and whose theories have been present in much recent Joyce criticism? This issue is critical to chapter 3, in which we find Stephen Dedalus in the process of acquiring or rejecting the discourse of his father. Like Freud, Lacan sees the castration complex as a critical developmental event. The child (subject) is split from the mother by the intervention of the father at this stage; the child enters the 'symbolic' order of spoken language and accepts the 'phallus' as 'transcendental signifier' of the law of the father. The threat of castration and selection of phallus as signifier, as well as the association of law and language with the father are appallingly male-centred. So is his concept of the mother's 'desire', which is a desire for the phallus, and a quality of lack or blankness unattractive to many feminists. On the other hand, Lacan does develop the pre-Oedipal stage, the role of the mother, and desire for her more extensively than Freud. The mother presides at the 'imaginary' stage preceding speech and at the 'mirror stage', when the child first senses separation from her. The subject suffers a sense of 'loss' of the mother after separation.

In her essay 'Castration or decapitation?' Cixous mockingly dismisses 'old' Lacan's 'strategy' of placing woman outside of law and language as a masculine myth. While men worry about and mourn the 'loss', she finds that women rebuild and express 'jouissance' (a concept of pleasure related to female sexuality).[24] Cixous invests mythical authority in the actions of maligned ancient mothers like Medusa, making castrated males like Oedipus look uninteresting in contrast.[25] These concepts will serve us in the revisionist myths of chapter 4, as well as Stephen's Oedipal conflicts, treated in chapter 3.

The most widely known feminist appropriation of Lacan has been made by Kristeva, who has allied herself more with male theory than Cixous, and who is decidedly out of sympathy with Cixous' mother myths. Her position is to accept the existence of a male-centred 'symbolic' order, and to work strategically to deconstruct it from the inside. Kristeva sees deconstructive work as a more advanced stage of feminism than the liberal pursuit of equality seen in the 1920s and still detectable in much Anglo-American feminism; she also resists the radical rejection of the male symbolic order which she equates with *écriture féminine*.[26] Kristeva focuses upon the pre-Oedipal phase, when the subject is in close relation to the mother, a mother who is not exclusively feminine, not a binary opposite to the father

of the symbolic stage. Her category of the 'semiotic' describes the discourse of this period of unified being with the
mother. In this phase, rhythmic, mobile pulsations are
gathered into 'provisional articulation' of *chora*, a term
borrowed from Plato, for whom it meant 'an invisible and
formless being'.[27] Kristeva redefines Plato's *chora* as a
'matrix space', playing with the same pun we have in chart-
ing feminist practices.[28] Thus Kristeva gives the mother a
more positive relation to language than Lacan, and she
develops origins of language that precede societal gender
differentiation. Such feminist revisions of binary logic,
semiotic language origins, and psychoanalytic myths of
family romance (focused here on relation to the mother),
will play essential roles in chapters 4 and 5.

The feminist questioning of binary logic can be seen as a
basic deconstruction of male-organized western thought.
The binary opposition of genders or sexes is derived from a
male symbolic order, according to Kristeva. At worst,
schemes of difference sustain degrading stereotypes used
historically to marginalize women, qualities an individual
critic may feel very distant to her identity. Thus Kristeva's
discussions of desire and *jouissance* have permitted female
identifications, but this is not a line she pursues. She suggests that, although the study of the female or the feminine
may place value on qualities that have been devalued in
male hegemony, the practice may involve the same old
hierarchical, trivializing game, making a scapegoat of the
male instead of the female. Gilbert and Gubar have shown
that Joyce is a likely candidate for this position. It is one he
understood, as he dramatized it in the topsy-turvy fates of
both Leopold Bloom in *Ulysses*, and HCE, the father figure
of *Finnegans Wake*.

Feminist Marxists are apt to be critical of attempts to
present women as a monolithic type, citing class, racial and
colonial factors of diversity. This might draw attention to
the danger of treating men, or male modernists as a unified
type as well. Less wedded to dialectics than their prede-
cessors, feminist Marxists comprehend gender in a system
of various oppressions and powers. We can examine Joyce

for non-deterministic concepts of gender, for sensitivity to
the comparability of gender, class and colonialism as issues
of power, for various 'economies' in art and life to which
feminist Marxists have alerted us, and we do so in chapter 5.

To finish, the title of this chapter, 'Plurabilities', invites
the issue of pluralism in feminist criticism in general, and
specifically in the methodology of this book. This stance has
proved controversial. Kolodny was severely criticized for
proposing a 'playful pluralism', an eclectic procedure that
would put her in touch with a corresponding pluralism in
contemporary, non-feminist criticism.[29] According to
Gayatri Spivak, this sort of pluralism is a capitulation:
'Pluralism is the method employed by the central authorities to neutralize opposition by seeming to accept it'[30].
Feminists trained in Marxism, psychoanalysis and linguistics tend toward more unified, systematic theory. But, as
exemplified earlier, there is a new tendency to superimpose
theoretical systems that their monological forefathers would
have privileged as self-sufficient. The Marxist Feminist
Collective uses what it calls a 'polylogic' in superimposing
psychoanalysis on Marxism.[31] The voice of their discourse
is a plural 'we'. The discourse of 'we' as opposed to egotistical 'I' was also explored by Woolf in the 1920s and 1930s.
She deliberately chooses a pluralistic project, inclusive of
positive as well as negative male writers, in the opening
pages of *A Room of One's Own*. Gynocriticism now adds a
dash of French feminism. Hélène Cixous, in describing
écriture féminine, emphasizes a plural 'inexhaustibility' of
phantasms in its unconscious female resources. Julia
Kristeva titled one book *Polylogues* (1977); she now encourages us to locate pluralism in the unconscious individual, whether the individual be male or female.[32] A final
endorsement of the plural approach comes from Joyce, who
introduced the term 'pollylogue' (*FW* 470.9), and used the
neologism that supplies our chapter title—'plurabilities'—
to describe Anna Livia Plurabelle, the maternal centre or
matrix space of *Finnegans Wake*.

CHAPTER TWO

The Canon: Challenges to Male-centred Literature and History

> Inverted volumes improperly arranged and not in the order of
> their common letters .... What reflection occupied him during
> the process of reversion of the inverted volumes? ... the de-
> ficient appreciation of literature possessed by females. (*U* 17.
> 1358-9, .1408-11)

To students today, James Joyce is one of the 'great writers'.
He appears in anthologies and on course lists; he is known
to educated people in the west and beyond. He has come to
represent the experimental prose of the modernist period of
literary history. In other words, Joyce is 'canonized'. The
canon we have today is largely the product of industries and
institutions dominated by men; it was composed by male
writers, centred upon men's experiences and views of history, and was more readily available to men than to women.
It leaves out a great deal that women have written and
largely writes and conceptualizes them out of history. The
academic canon exists alongside popular literature, and we
will briefly consider what was commonly read in Joyce's
Dublin. Canonization has become one of the most lively
feminist-inspired issues in the academy today, and provides
an accessible and highly relevant start to our feminist excursion into Joyce. In this chapter, we will be operating in the
upper, or conscious, realist range of feminist theories
grounded in the matrix of chapter 1, drawing upon Virginia
Woolf's early analysis of these problems in *A Room of One's*

Own, as well as the feminist approaches of gynocriticism, mainstreaming and feminist Marxism. Our consideration of popular literature, in which heroines and women writers figured importantly, will be assisted by recent studies of female romances, or heroines' texts.

Paradoxically, Joyce's present availability owes much to the industry and support of women in publishing. Joyce's nurturing by females was not just a fortunate fall into female altruism. He was selected from other modernists because the women involved found revolutionary affinities in Joyce. Joyce began under male patronage—his father's. John Joyce had his son's poem on Charles Stuart Parnell published privately. Presumably, it echoed the father's sense of history. Next, the prestigious British periodical, *The Fortnightly Review*, published his review on Ibsen (1900). With the exception of the relatively conventional poems in *Chamber Music* (1907), Joyce's increasingly experimental and iconoclastic works met with rejections. *St Stephen's*, his college newspaper, censored his attack on the Irish literary revival, 'The Day of the Rabblement', and Joyce published it privately with an equally marginal essay on women's education by Irish feminist and friend, Francis Skeffington. The bourgeois readers of *The Irish Homestead* objected to the stories that became *Dubliners*, so publication ceased after three. With *Dubliners* still unpublished, Joyce's prospects for *A Portrait* seemed gloomy until Ezra Pound put him in touch with the daring women editors of *The Egoist*. Dora Marsden and Harriet Shaw Weaver were willing to deal with printers' fears of litigation, to defy the norms of established literature and the economics of the marketplace, as were other female editors of small, individualist magazines.

The gynocritical concept of a muted female culture applies well to the operations of women editors and publishers of Joyce. *The Egoist* was descended from suffragist periodicals (*The Freewoman,* later renamed *The New Freewoman*), and staffed by feminists, including Rebecca West, H.D., and Bryher (Winnifred Ellermann). As writers, these women were neglected during the years when

Joyce studies grew into an industry, but their muted
modernist tradition has drawn the attention of feminist
critics and publishers in the last five years.[1] Joyce was living
in Trieste when his work began appearing in *The Egoist*,
and the only woman connected with the enterprise that he
came to know personally was Weaver. If so disposed, he
could have read the work of Weaver, West and H.D. in *The
Egoist*.

Weaver re-made the quaint role of literary patronage in a
style of her own, learned partially from her participation in
Victorian women's roles. She avoided poses of authority
and airs of social superiority, offering instead common
sense, practical nurture, and the psychological support that
came from utter dependability and loyalty. Weaver's
support of Joyce began with handling the details of periodical publication of *A Portrait*, including the same sort of
haggling with printers that so delayed *Dubliners*. She
eventually changed from periodical publishing to book
publishing. The Egoist Press was established 'on non-
commercial lines' with the aim of making 'operative an
influence capable of transforming our entire world of form-
thought and action'.[2] Its Joyce list included several editions
of *A Portrait*, as well as English editions of *Ulysses, Exiles,
Dubliners,* and *Chamber Music*. Weaver also published
T.S. Eliot, Wyndham Lewis, Ezra Pound, Marianne
Moore, H.D. and Dora Marsden, a list with a generous
presence of women writers.

With Paris as his home for most of the time from 1920
until his death, Joyce entered a rare time and place for
women, focused for him during the critical early years by
'Shakespeare and Company', the bookshop of American
emigrée Sylvia Beach. Paris of the 1920s was honeycombed
with women's communities, each with a space and personality of its own.[3] There was a cosmopolitan blending of
writers and artists, as well as experiments in lifestyle.
Lesbian *ménages* like that of Sylvia Beach and French
bookseller Adrienne Monnier or Gertrude Stein and Alice
B. Toklas were not unusual, though their sexual orientation
was not universally known. As booksellers, Beach and

Monnier were as unconventional as the editors of *The Egoist*. Monnier describes the atmosphere of her bookshop in terms appropriate to female culture, where personal interactions and domestic arts are emphasized: The shop is 'a place of transition between street and house', and 'a true magic chamber' where the 'stranger', given access to books, becomes understood as a 'soul'.[4] We might see Beach's bookshop as an updated amalgamation of the eighteenth-century coffee house and the bluestocking's salon. When other efforts, including Weaver's in England, failed to secure publication of *Ulysses,* the shop became the outlet and office of a publishing house, and even an agency for typists, many of them female. Joyce came to the canon, then, with substantial though marginal and unconventional forms of female assistance.

Canonical status is not permanent. Reputations have always risen and fallen in response to critical currents and ideologies. Today, the feminist critics interested in women writers and in mainstreaming women's studies perspectives are challenging the composition of the canon, and even the desirability of canonization. Catharine Stimpson asks why Joyce should receive so much attention in scholarly journals across the political spectrum, while the comparably experi-mental poet, Gertrude Stein, has not been repeatedly and patiently deciphered.[5] Only Virginia Woolf has attained canonical status, manifested by her presence in widely-used anthologies and on course lists, and this has come recently. Feminist publishers like Virago, The Women's Press and The Feminist Press have returned modernist women writers to print in economical paperbacks, and their success has encouraged established houses like Viking-Penguin and Norton to join in the enterprise. Neglected genres in which women have specialized are becoming increasingly available; important texts include the early journalism of Rebecca West, the multi-volume editions of Woolf's diaries and letters, and the biographical fiction and epic poetry of H.D. The old canon is pressured, as always, by contemporary writing, much of it by women. Women now play roles in fiction not available to them in the culture of Joyce's era.

There are more black, third world and lesbian writers openly treating cultural difference. There are the women writers of the *écriture féminine* school. How will Joyce fare in re-evaluations of the canon and canonization? As noted in chapter 1, Joyce is in danger of becoming the scapegoat of female modernism, of playing the role Milton did in Gilbert and Gubar's *The Madwoman in the Attic*. I think Joyce's own literary treatment of the very problems of canonization may in part determine his future.

As male *bildung*, Joyce's early realistic works give us opportunities to enter the classroom or to otherwise draw inferences about the nature of the canon experienced by his young male characters. Joyce was schooled in all-male classically and theologically oriented institutions from the age of six. Whenever possible, his family chose the Jesuits, the highest class of Catholic educators, whose methodology imitated medieval scholasticism, an argumentative, rational system of precise definitions, discriminations, enumerated aspects and allusions to authorities far removed from the female styles introduced in chapter 1. Their teaching was a blend of catechism, sermon and pseudo-Socratic dialogue. In the Literary and Historical Society of University College, Dublin, the young men (including Joyce) demonstrated their oratorical and critical skills in debates and vehement discussions of formal papers. Although the Jesuits resisted outside influences on their curriculum, yearly competitive exhibitions and the public examinations of the Royal University encouraged a factual, names-and-dates form of study focused upon great historical and literary figures. This blended with Jesuit catechism, nineteenth-century science and positivist philosophy to constitute a factual, rational, hierarchical, classical, male-centred academic discourse.

Joyce learned these modes of thought and performance well. Yet in his writing, he could distance himself by placing a persona (a fictional character comparable to but not identical to himself) in the position of learner. Joyce explored alternatives to the rational tradition of canonized great men and allowed his personas (often naïvely) to do the same. These alternatives often drew upon female sub-culture, which posed serious challenges to the classical curriculum.

In *A Portrait of the Artist as a Young Man*, Stephen Dedalus begins early to absorb the lessons on the Romans, the Greeks and Napoleon. He thinks that there are right answers about history, and examples of greatness to be followed, even in family life. There should be simple mono-logical solutions to problems involving gender, like the question posed by the bully, Wells, 'Do you kiss your mother before you go to bed?' (*P* 14). Personal application of male historical paradigms is evident in the aftermath of the pandy-bat incident. A priest has beaten Stephen's hand as punishment for Stephen's having broken his glasses. The dynamics of phallic power over excised or castrated vision invite gender-based interpretations, but the boys cannot articulate them. Stephen's peers state his grievance in classical historical terms: 'The senate and the Roman people declare that Dedalus has been wrongly punished'. Stephen responds:

> He would go up and tell the rector that he had been wrongly punished. A thing like that had been done before by somebody in history, by some great person whose head was in the books of history .... Those were the great men whose names were in Richmal Magnall's Questions. History was all about those men and what they did and that was what Peter Parley's Tales about Greece and Rome were all about. (53-4)

On his way to secure justice from the highest school auth-ority, Stephen displays internalized male-biased values that allow him to feel superior to his punisher. His name, Dedalus, connects him to the great men of the classics he has studied: 'The great men in the history had names like that and nobody made fun of them .... Dolan: it was like the name of a woman that washed clothes' (55). Stephen has learned that women in domestic service deserve low regard; great men in history are respectable. Joyce was not finished with washerwomen, however, as we shall see in analysis of *Finnegans Wake* in chapter 4.

Stephen develops a reputation as a prize-winning student over the years. His memory is excellent; his knowledge of the catechism can be used later to divert a priestly instructor from unprepared lessons (105). The Jesuits of Belvedere are convinced that they have a potential recruit (105). But long before he must use a 'habit of quiet obedience' to disguise other interests from the priests, the young Stephen searches out different angles, de-centring Jesuit-style learning. Stephen tries, but only half-heartedly, to compete on one of two teams named (with significant indifference to Irish nationalism) for the historical English factions of York and Lancaster in the Wars of the Roses. Due to illness, Stephen's mind works feverishly, eluding a more customary discipline. On a more normal day, Stephen had listed his name at the head of a hierarchy, ranging from self to universe (16). But on this day, Stephen's mind wanders from manly competition to colour, rearranging and inventing. Stephen displays little respect for the hierarchy of colours accorded to high and low places. He thinks of the flower (usually a female emblem) originally attached to the colour symbolism. He introduces off-shades and plays with a chiasmic structure (parallelism in reverse order that achieves symmetry rather than hierarchy): 'White roses and red roses: those were beautiful colours to think of. And the cards for first place and second place and third place were beautiful colours too: pink and cream and lavender. Lavender and cream and pink roses were beautiful to think of' (12). At his second school, Belvedere, Stephen cannot attend to a typical history lesson; he is troubled by the concentration on names which veil and mute what interests him: 'royal persons, favourites, intriguers, bishops passed like mute phantoms behind their veil of names' (123). His mind is diverted at this time by his own mysteries—a sense of sin with a prostitute, and concern for his soul, problems we will return to in chapter 4 (125). Stephen grows more openly critical of the educational process at University College. He cuts his English lecture, but imagines his peers at their Jesuit rituals, their heads 'meekly bent as they wrote in their notebooks the points they were bidden to note,

nominal definitions, essential definitions and examples or
dates of birth or death, chief works' and so on (177-8).
Stephen turns the available instruction toward a different
form of history. He seeks social rather than political,
militant history, often finding his cues in language, however
ill-chosen by his instructors:

> The crises and victories and secessions in Roman history were
> handed on to him in the trite words *in tanto discrimine* and he
> had tried to peer into the social life of the city of cities through
> the words *implere ollam denariorum* which the rector had
> rendered sonorously as the filling of a pot with denaries. (179)

His new history of pots rather than battles has affinity with
feminist history, as defined by feminist historians like
Gerda Lerner. *Ulysses* offers many discussions of military
engagements, but Stephen figures in them peripherally, if
at all. He is less involved in the historical debates of the
'Eumaeus' episode than is Leopold Bloom, though they
agree momentarily on the values of pacifism. As if to
emphasize his distaste for the subject, he requests, rather
affectedly, 'O, oblige me by taking away that knife. I can't
look at the point of it. It reminds me of Roman history' (*U*
16. 814-6).

Stephen's educational experiences as a young student are
echoed in the first three stories of *Dubliners*, where the
central intelligence is also a bright young boy. A direct
challenge to a classical curriculum is posed by popular literature in 'An Encounter'. The schoolboy protagonist and his
friend Mahoney in effect reject the dull school curriculum
in favour of adventure. The story begins with a lesson in
Roman history, interrupted by Father Butler's discovery
that one boy is reading a rival text, a wild-west pulp thriller
titled *The Apache Chief*. This attack on the canon, by
stories made available cheaply by the popular press, is fended
off by the priest with a battery of moral, intellectual and class
biases: 'The man who wrote it, I suppose, was some wretched
scribbler that writes these things for a drink. I'm surprised
at boys like you, educated, reading such stuff. I could
understand it if you were . . . National School boys' (*D* 20).

The boy has a different preference for cheap reading—detective fiction—and struggles with a sense of difference from the other boys, even in their alliance against the Priest's approved texts:

> We banded ourselves together, some boldly, some in jest and some almost in fear: and of the number of these latter, the reluctant Indians who were afraid to seem studious or lacking in robustness, I was one. The adventures . . . of the Wild West were remote from my nature but, at least, they opened doors of escape. I liked better some American detective stories which were traversed from time to time by unkempt fierce and beautiful girls. (20)

The boy feels less virile and less inclined toward war play than his companions. He substitutes a genre with greater intellectual challenge and the fantasy of girls who are not only beautiful, but 'fierce' and 'unkempt'. Unlike girls in his actual experience, these display power and violate the cultural norm of grooming. Girls figure less in both the priest's canon and the wild west alternative. It is likely that some of his detective fiction would have had female authors, and he would have shared them with a female readership. Joyce's boy characters do not read romances with central heroines, but these equally non-canonical texts would have been comparably produced and priced.[6]

Actual females figure only minimally in 'An Encounter'. Mrs Dillon is so marginal as to exist only in a 'peaceful odour' left behind in the hall, which the boy remarks in the first paragraph of the story. Mother odours are also remarkable to young Stephen Dedalus in *A Portrait*. Mrs Dillon seems to offer remote mystery, but, like many women in *Dubliners*, she is invisible, withdrawn to the church. The boy is detached in attitude from a group of girls he and Mahoney encounter in a lower-class neighbourhood, offering no protest when Mahoney chases them; the girls are defended by boys of their own class in this miniature study of gender and power in class hierarchies.

The 'old josser' takes the place of Father Butler as instructor at the end of 'An Encounter'. His literary canon is not the classics offered by the priests, but his pederastic and homosexual tendencies are reminiscent of the homosexual contexts of boys' education in classical Athens. His canon includes romantic writers popular with the Irish adult public, Thomas Moore and Walter Scott; but it ends with 'Lord Lytton', Edward Bulwer-Lytton, whose romances included violence and terror, and who is on Molly Bloom's reading list in *Ulysses*. Like the priest, the 'josser' uses upper-class identifications as part of his appeal. Lytton is, after all, a 'Lord'. The man encourages the narrator to feel superior to Mahoney since he is a 'bookworm' while Mahoney wields a catapult. The boy notices the man's 'good accent'. But he also begins to notice problems with his talk, which is circular and repetitive. Girls are not just a subject of interest, as were the girls of detective fiction to the boy. They are the obsession around which his talk revolves. The strange man wants to know about the boy's 'sweethearts' and dwells on physical aspects of white hands and soft hair (25). His sexual arousal from this talk is evident in his shivering and his eventual need to do something 'queer' in the field. When he returns, his new preoccupation is whipping young boys for having sweethearts (27). Clearly, this is not the alternative the boy had been seeking. He must fall back on alliance with a virile male, Mahoney, to escape, but this is no solution either. The strange man of 'An Encounter' has aesthetic interests that Joyce entertained repeatedly, however. The feminine attribute of white hands pervades *A Portrait*; the admired hair is a motif of *Chamber Music*; the circular narrative is the ultimate design of *Finnegans Wake*.

Episode 2 of *Ulysses*, 'Nestor', gives us an opportunity to see how an older Stephen Dedalus conducts a teaching situation. In the schema Joyce gave Stuart Gilbert for *Ulysses*, 'catechism' is the technique of the chapter, and 'history' is its 'art'.[7] As an interim teacher, Stephen is probably not responsible for the curriculum he teaches. It begins with Roman political history—memorized answers to questions about a famous battle. Stephen moves on to a canonized literary figure, Milton, apparently having assigned the memorization of 'Lycidas'. Though the texts are standard, Stephen's pedagogy is lax and unconventional. He aids a student who is furtively glancing at his text, and allows de-centring of the historical subject. Stephen pursues the pun 'pier' offered by an unprepared student who has no interest in the identity of the Roman general Pyrrhus. He senses when his students' thoughts have turned to girls, prompted by a reference to a typical trysting place, Kingstown Pier. Stephen imagines their thoughts: 'Edith, Ethel, Gerty, Lily. Their likes: their breaths, too, sweetened with tea and jam, their bracelets tittering in the struggle' (*U* 2.36-8). There are many possibilities for female intertextuality here—sweet female odour reminiscent of 'An Encounter', becomes a leitmotif of *Ulysses*. Another 'Gerty' provides diversion for Bloom in the 'Nausicaa' episode. A tittering, flirtatious girl appeared at the close of 'Araby', where earlier Mangan's sister 'turned a silver bracelet' and diverted the boy from school and male friends (*D* 32, 30). 'Lily' on Stephen's list recalls the servant girl of 'The Dead', who disrupts Gabriel's control of the evening at its very start. In the classroom scene, Stephen is hardly master of his history; he has to check his book for the location of a battle that his student cannot recall. Stephen later describes history as 'a nightmare from which I am trying to awake' (*U* 2.377) to his employer, Mr Deasy. As Stephen's students fail at their standard lessons, he reflects inwardly about the distortions and failures of history itself, and its possible alternatives:

> Fabled by the daughters of memory. And yet it was in some way if not as memory fabled it. A phrase, then, of impatience, thud of Blake's wings of excess. I hear the ruin of all space, shattered glass and toppling masonry, and time one livid final flame. What's left us then? (2.7-10)

Memory becomes muse in Stephen's literary imagination, and both have failed, though memory used to be Stephen's *forte*. Edmund Epstein suggests that the failure offers an alternative in Blakeian vision.[8] Blake's revolutionary 'Proverbs of Hell' challenge canonical and traditional moral and cultural values. But, as evidenced in the later 'Scylla and Charybdis' episode, Stephen has a stronger allegiance to the more traditional Aristotle, whose ideas of history permeate the passage.

Stephen finds recorded history random. His student's quotation is 'that phrase the world had remembered'. History and time starkly reduce 'infinite possibilities': The deaths of Pyrrhus and Caesar 'are not to be thought away. Time has branded them and fettered they are lodged in the room of the infinite possibilities they have ousted.' Stephen wonders, 'Can those have been possible seeing that they never were? Or was that only possible which came to pass?' (2.48-52). In reconsidering Aristotle, Stephen is groping toward mental and imaginative expression of the possible which was never recorded. Later, in the midst of his exposition on Shakespeare in the 'Scylla and Charybdis' episode, Stephen expands on history: 'what Caesar would have lived to do had he believed the soothsayer: what might have been: possibilities of the possible as possible: things not known: what name Achilles bore when he lived among women' (9.347-51). The last thought suggests that in a woman's sub-culture (Achilles among women), there is a different form of naming, unknown to historicized, recorded literature. Joyce is still working on the problem of the possible in *Finnegans Wake*, where he imagines a place, 'Isitachapel-Asitalucin ... where the possible was the improbable and the improbable the inevitable' (110.8-12). The place has a female association, Issy, the daughter figure of the *Wake*, and the passage parodies 'Harrystotalics' rhetoric.

Stephen, the historical canon he teaches, and his interaction with Mr Deasy draw our attention to battles, contests, deaths, a history that is severely confining for the individuals involved, and inadequately recollected by the memory. Norms of battle, joust, race become metaphors for life in the classroom, the meeting of young girls and boys is a 'struggle'. The imaginative power of this form of education is shown in the 'Circe' episode, when 'A BLUECOAT SCHOOLBOY' comes forth to utter his 'bravo!' to a history of international wars and Irish risings (15.1525-36). Women are written into history by misogynists like Mr Deasy as agents of destruction of the male order.

In 'Nestor' Stephen records an alternate drama of a sort not usually chronicled in history. It is the nurturing of the pathetic student, Sargent, by *'Amor matris*: subjective and objective genitive' (2.165-6): 'But for her the race of the world would have trampled him under foot, a squashed boneless snail' (2.141-2). Stephen here takes up the discussion of mother love begun by his friend Cranly at the close of *A Portrait*, embracing it only after the intervening death of his own mother has ousted new possibilities with her. Mrs Dedalus' prostrate body and fire-consumed skeleton inject themselves into Stephen's thoughts about Sargent, and guilt about his treatment of her haunts Stephen through the 'Circe' episode, which we will turn to in chapter 4. In 'Nestor' her body is surmounted by 'fiery Columbanus'. This is appropriate to a woman consumed by both saint and son, and subordinated by the church as well as the pen. Stephen gives Sargent careless nurture, but is more occupied by his own comparable past.

Stephen's students divert the lesson from the canon. He meets their request for a story with a riddle, a sub-literary form more closely associated with women's realm of the nursery than with the classroom:

> *The cock crew*
> *The sky was blue;*
> *The bells in heaven*
> *Were striking eleven.*
> *Tis time for this poor soul*
> *To go to heaven.* (2.102-7)

The answer is 'the fox burying his grandmother under a hollybush' (2.115), and this is a personally significant perplexity that comes back to Stephen incessantly throughout the day. Stephen later juxtaposes the 'poor soul gone to heaven' with his mother, who 'had gone, scarcely having been'. The male fox is elaborated: 'on a heath beneath winking stars a fox, red reek of rapine in his fur, with

merciless bright eyes scraped in the earth, listened, scraped
up the earth, listened, scraped and scraped' (2.147-50).
The fox is a significant identification for Stephen as he
works furtively, perhaps from guilt, to bury his failure
with his mother, now seen as a victim of figurative rape.[9]
'Cunning' was one of the methods Stephen chose for himself at the end of A Portrait. Stephen tries to bury his past
and move on, but he also keeps scraping back over it.
'Rapine' offers a metaphor of the historical treatment
of women, the lower class and the colonies, as well as
their minimal rendering in history. The torturing, nerve-
wracking scraping and scraping of the female earth by the
fox is appropriate to the act of rape. The fox buries his
'grandmother', so in addition to Stephen's mother we
should consider a more remote past, a lost wisdom, gram-
mar and language, silenced now while the male 'cock crew'.
History has been limiting, assaulting, murdering. In the
'Hades' episode, Bloom recalls an equally grotesque drama,
worthy of his gothic tastes, involving sexual assault in death:
'And even scraping up the earth at night with a lantern like
that case I read of to get at fresh buried females or even
putrefied with running gravesores' (6.997-9). The burial
Stephen portrays in 'Nestor' is not final, however. Situated
near the holly bush, it offers compost for spiritual rebirth,
the female, berry-laden holly serving as an emblem of
Christmas.[10] In effect, Stephen replaces history with a
perplexing riddle that opens out into multiple allegorical
interpretations, suggested above. Perhaps Joyce is fleeing
history; modernists have been suspected of evading it. But
more significantly, he may be searching for a form that
demands more than recorded fact, presumed greatness, or
singular solution. In the riddle of 'Nestor', and Stephen's
mental elaborations of it, Joyce explores the process of
burial and the multiple potentials of recovery—plot
elements that will recur in the myths we consider in
chapter 4.

Stephen's major performance in Ulysses is the exposition
of a theory on Hamlet, most canonized of secular texts, in
the 'Scylla and Charybdis' episode. The concept of canon-

ized male greatness is advanced by Stephen and respected by his Anglo-Irish literary audience. Stephen informs us that 'A man of genius makes no mistakes' (9.228). Æ (George Russell), Thomas Lyster and John Eglinton all refer to Shakespeare as a great man among other greats like Goethe (9.2-3, .181, .359). The listeners are also interested in 'becoming important' as Irish writers (9.312-13). Stephen summons his backgrounds in Aristotle and Ignatius Loyola to launch his theory: 'Unsheathe your dagger definitions' (9.84); 'Composition of place. Ignatius Loyola, make haste to help me!' (9.163). The summons of a sainted male mentor bears some resemblance to Stephen's invocation of Daedalus at the close of *A Portrait*. The phallic dagger suggests verbal violence.

Stephen begins his exposition with the ghost of a father figure (9.147), a strange concentration for a young man so beset by the ghost of a mother. His theory re-creates male-centred, Biblical concepts of the consubstantiality of the father and the son, and of male succession, even deposing the Virgin Mary from the prominence she had achieved in the Catholic Church.

> —A father, Stephen said, battling against hopelessness, is a necessary evil. . . . Fatherhood, in the sense of conscious beget-ing, is unknown to man. It is a mystical estate, an apostolic succession, from only begetter to only begotten. On that mys-tery and not on the madonna . . . the church is founded and founded irremovably because founded, like the world, macro and microcosm, upon the void. (9.828-43)

Consubstantial male succession establishes an immortal form of communication, 'a voice heard only in the heart of him who is the substance of his shadow, the son consub-stantial with the father' (9.480-1). But it also establishes poignant rivalry and strict sexual sundering in the dread of combined incest and homosexuality: 'They are sundered by a bodily shame so steadfast that the criminal annals of the world, stained with all other incests and bestialities, hardly records its breach. . . . He is a new male: his growth is his father's decline, his youth his father's envy, his friend his father's enemy' (9.850-7). Fraternal rivalry is manifested in his brothers' possible cuckolding of him.

Unlike Virginia Woolf, Stephen Dedalus never entertains the notion that Shakespeare might have had a sister with literary talents comparable to his own.[11] He dismisses the 'boywomen' of Shakespeare as 'the women of a boy. Their life, thought, speech are lent them by males' (9.254-5). Stephen does have a female focus though. He studies the 'boldfaced Stratford wench' (9.259-60), later the adulterous wife, Ann Hathaway. The sub-text of her wooing Shakespeare, their sundering, and his recovery of what he had lost in his daughter's child, underlies Shakespeare's mature works, according to Stephen's theory. Ann's sub-text goes beyond the simple role of virgin–whore of the traditional popular romance, which ends in marriage. There is an element of patriarchal punishment, perhaps for sexual exploits, in the bequest of the second-best bed, which so interests Stephen's audience.[12] Stephen wants to find an Ann and a Perdita, it seems, 'And my turn? When?' he thinks (9.261). Ann has the initiative to seek out her young lover; she inspires and betrays him, and lives on. She might remind us of the fiesty heroines of the detective narratives favoured in 'An Encounter'. Perdita, the granddaughter, suggests an alternative to patrilineal concerns.

> —Will he not see reborn in her, with the memory of his own youth added, another image?
>
> Do you know what you are talking about? Love, yes. Word known to all men . . . .
>
> —His own image to a man with that queer thing genius is the standard of all experience, material and moral. Such an appeal will touch him. The images of other males of his blood will repel him. He will see in them grotesque attempts of nature to foretell or to repeat himself. (9.427-35)

Stephen feels that the line of female descent (from Ann, to daughter to granddaughter) is less competitive to a man than a line of male descent, and is founded upon love. In the 'Cyclops' chapter, tribal male lineage is parodied (12.1124). Female descent alone survives in the Bloom family through Milly Bloom. In 'Scylla and Charybdis', Stephen repeats the observation from 'Nestor', '*Amor matris*, subjective and objective genitive, may be the only true thing in life', in the midst of his thinking about paternity's being founded upon the void (9.843-4). While this theory remains centred in the male's experience, it does lend immediate importance to mother and wife, associating life and love, 'the word known to all men' with them.[13] Stephen imagines female indifference to Shakespeare himself, when early in his exposition he imagines Shakespeare walking through Stratford: '—Shakespeare has left the Huguenot's house in Silver street and walks by the swan-mews along the riverbank. But he does not stay to feed the pen chivying her game of cygnets toward the rushes. The swan of Avon has other thoughts' (9.158-60). By *Finnegans Wake,* a hen has texts, as well as thoughts, as we shall see in chapter 5. Stephen's family-centred interpretation of Shakespeare offends listeners more accustomed to considering genius apart from life.

Though Stephen is indebted to classicism and scholasticism, and though he makes the canonized British master, Shakespeare, the subject of his central literary discourse in *Ulysses*, these authorities receive significant challenges from Stephen, his audience, and Joyce, as the arranger of *Ulysses*. Stephen is not even prepared to say he believes in the theories he expresses on Shakespeare. In *A Portrait*, Stephen acknowledges weariness after searching the 'spectral words of Aristotle and Aquinas', and is relieved by 'the dainty songs of the Elizabethans', and gladdened by his passage through 'the squalor and noise and sloth of the city', (*P* 176). Stephen is 'disheartened' by 'the firm dry tone' of the dean of studies, outlining a Jesuitical method of exploring beauty through a set of distinctions (189-91). He is not eager to become an 'unlit lamp' or a 'faithful servingman of the knightly Loyola' (190).

Clearly without Jesuit endorsement, Stephen had sought out romantic texts like Dumas' *The Count of Monte Cristo.* One appeal of these texts was their romantic visions of women like Mercedes. Stephen has prized other romantic writers who offer comparable distanced female inspirational figures for questing. Foremost is Byron, who provides the form for Stephen's poem to E.C. (70), and for whom Stephen sustains a beating by virile schoolfellows. Byron had been denounced by Stephen's Jesuit instructor as immoral and heretical.

In Blake, Stephen encountered a profoundly radical critique of cultural hegemony, one which contributed to his re-vision of history, as we have seen in 'Nestor'. 'The most enlightened of Western poets' referred to in an essay Joyce wrote in 1902 was Blake, according to Joyce's brother, Stanislaus (CW 74-5). Interestingly, Blake was ensconced alongside Joyce in Sylvia Beach's bookshop. The romantic temper, with its heritage of the French Revolution, its denial of hierarchies, and its greater interest in subjective and unconscious human experience, added new dimensions to Joyce and to his persona, which brought him closer to the sensibilities of revolutionary women writers like Mary Wollstonecraft, Mary Shelley and Charlotte Brontë.

Even in his pursuit of classical male writers, Stephen adopted his own course. The final chapter of A Portrait shows Stephen de-centring classical teaching to suit his interests. He reads Ovid and Horace with the Jesuits, but is distracted by the whimsical words used to translate Ovid and by the human imprint of the 'timeworn pages' of his copy of Horace (P 179). In John Henry Newman, Stephen admires a writer approved for the modern Jesuit canon, but values, not the theology, but the 'silver-veined prose'. Stephen also seeks out the heretics of ecclesiastical history. He defends Bruno of Nola to the dean of students, just as he had defended Byron with his contemporaries. Stephen is not physically punished for this allegiance, but he reminds the dean that Bruno was brutally burned. In a book review on Bruno (1903), Joyce agrees with the author's view of Bruno as a revisionist of scholasticism. Joyce appreciates Bruno's pluralist attitude—a position of significance in the feminist questions addressed in chapter 1. Bruno's system has various poles, 'by turns rationalist and mystic, theistic and pantheistic'. Joyce reiterates Coleridge's identification of Bruno as a 'dualist' (*CW* 133-4). Thus Bruno offers a greater sensitivity to alternative paradigms than the more monological scholastic thinking, but we should recall that dualistic thinking is also suspect as a male-generated paradigm by Marxist and post-structuralist feminists. Where Brunonian binaries operate in Joyce, their function must be deconstructed; where they are synthetic or question the usual hierarchy, they may offer a positive paradigm. Bruno's supposed abhorrence of the multitude is endorsed by Joyce in 'The Day of the Rabblement'. This supports the pose of aloof, romantic artist, and is more difficult to accommodate to a feminist position. The multitude scorned by Bruno and Joyce, however, may be most objectionable for its mindless support of hegemonic culture.

Stephen's thoughts are also crossed by the modern continental playwrights, Gerhart Hauptmann and Henrik Ibsen, who are serious alternatives to the classical curriculum of the Jesuit university. Interestingly, Joyce specialized, not in the classics but in modern literature, the subject usually chosen by female students. Ibsen has surprisingly little place in *A Portrait*, considering Joyce's substantial effort to claim his place in the dramatic canon in such essays as 'Drama and Life', 'Ibsen's New Drama', 'Catalina', and 'The Day of the Rabblement'. Joyce's major performance at the university was not on the well-canonized Shakespeare, Stephen's choice for the library discourse, but on Ibsen. In 'Drama and Life', Joyce notes that the 'Shakespearean clique' had toppled an already failing classical dramatic tradition. Yet he sets about dismissing Shakespeare in turn, finding him a writer of 'literature in dialogue'. Ibsen is preferable as a writer of a higher and more collective 'dramatic' art (*CW* 39, 45ff.). Stephen's few thoughts on Hauptmann and Ibsen suggest that they provide him with images and attitudes not available in the canon. Thoughts of Hauptmann come to Stephen from the sensuous 'rain-laden trees', evocative of the girls and women in his plays. Ibsen is a revolutionary 'spirit' that 'would blow through him like a keen wind, a spirit of wayward boyish beauty' (*P* 176). Joyce uses 'keen air' to describe the effect of female characters in his essay, 'Ibsen's New Drama' (*CW* 65); Stephen transforms the female character into 'boyish' form (see *J & F* 47-53).

Stephen is not the only character in *A Portrait* and *Ulysses* who would pose a challenge to the established canon. Buck Mulligan constantly reminds us of the challenge of the aesthetes, and the label is used for Stephen several times in *Ulysses*. Mulligan's odd combination of materialism with neo-Hellenism undermines classicism rather than reviving it.

The Irish literary revival presents another challenge to the classics but it was a challenge that left Joyce profoundly ambivalent. There are tantalizing parallels between Ireland's efforts to recover a lost literature and the feminist gyno-critic's efforts to claim a muted female literary tradition. Representatives of the Irish revival exclude Stephen from their evening gathering at George Moore's house, even as they repeatedly interrupt his Shakespearean discourse. Æ, Yeats and other members of the Irish literary movement received mental debunking from Stephen in 'Scylla and Charybdis', but Stephen is haunted throughout the day by Yeats' lyric 'Who goes with Fergus'. Joyce enjoyed presenting James Clarence Mangan as a writer neglected in the Irish canon, and suggested his ostracism was due to Irish social attitudes (*CW* 176). To Joyce, one of Mangan's most notable achievements was a female 'imaginative personality reflecting the light of imaginative beauty', a 'chivalrous ideal' (*CW* 78-9). Indeed, Irish writers like Mangan, Moore and Yeats were as capable as Dumas of providing Joyce with female ideals for male romantic quest. Stephen regards Ireland's national poet, Thomas Moore, as a 'Firbolg', one of the early, earthy peoples who occupied Ireland before the supposedly grander Milesians (*P* 180). Yet he repeatedly thinks of his songs, and even sings his and others' Irish lyrics upon the request of a young woman (*P* 219). Stephen is attracted to a servant girl's singing of 'Sweet Rosie O'Grady', though he guards his response with an Aristotelian demand to see Rosie, and with a distracting Latin observation *mulier cantat* (*P* 244). In his early essays Joyce proposes a new literature for Ireland that builds upon past traditions and international models. He remarks in 'The Day of the Rabblement', 'A nation which never advanced so far as a miracle-play affords no literary model to the artist' (*CW* 70). Accordingly, he looked toward the Continent, instead of back into the Irish folk for his models. His aloof attitude and missionary role were patriarchal, yet the social theory he encountered in Ibsen and Hauptmann was far more revolutionary than anything literary Ireland offered.

It does not seem to occur to Stephen Dedalus that a female literary tradition might also offer alternatives to the original canon presented in his schooling. 'Oxen of the Sun', the episode of *Ulysses* that purports to trace literary history, and another occasion for academic performance, is silent on the novel as a genre identified with women writers. To Woolf, this was a revolutionary moment of women's history: 'Towards the end of the eighteenth century a change came about which if I were rewriting history, I should describe more fully and think of greater importance than the Crusades or the Wars of the Roses. The middle-class woman began to write.'[14] 'Oxen' is not necessarily an honour roll. Dickens might just as soon have been omitted as parodied, but his presence bespeaks his canonical importance. In a survey of prose of the eras when we most expect women writers (the seventeenth century onward), Joyce presents Bunyan, Pepys, Defoe, Swift, Addison, Sterne, Gibbon, Charles Lamb, De Quincey, Landor, Newman, Pater, Ruskin and Carlyle. The gothic novel, a special province of women writers, has Sheridan Le Fanu as its representative, though this is perhaps a biographical artifact, since Joyce's father owned the novel cited. Joyce's apparent use of anthologies by Saintsbury and Peacock, which may have influenced the selection, only serves to emphasize the exclusion of women writers from the working canon of literary history.[15]

For years, Woolf's literary historical fantasy novel, *Orlando* (1928), was dismissed as a *roman à clef*, or a rest between the more demanding work of *To the Lighthouse* and *The Waves*. It coincides, however, with her serious critical re-evaluation of gender and literature, *A Room of One's Own*. As a treatment of the social and gender implications of literature, *Orlando* has emerged in feminist criticism as a revolutionary work. 'Oxen of the Sun' has never been a favoured episode of *Ulysses*.[16] Gilbert and Gubar correctly focus on it as a highly problematic text.[17] In my interpretation of literary modernism, *Orlando*, with its exuberant androgynous protagonist, whose gender is altered to most deeply elicit the literary politics of collective cultural ages, is more worthy of canonization.

Although Stephen Dedalus makes considerable challenges to the classical literary and historical canons on which he was reared, the manner of Stephen's critique remains questionable. In his literary arguments, Stephen subscribes to hierarchical judgements and mentions only male writers, an arrangement directly comparable to the early model of great men in history which he absorbed and personalized. Stephen may substitute what figures he values, but they remain male and are set in competition for the first place. The same practice is visible in Joyce's essays, like 'James Clarence Mangan' and 'The Day of the Rabblement'. The latter is packed with allusions to contemporary writers, all masterfully ranked (*CW* 70-1). In 'Scylla and Charybdis' Stephen's audience is entirely male, as were the auditors of his aesthetics in *A Portrait*. Though young women students have begun to come to the library, they have not yet penetrated to the librarians' inner sanctum, where Stephen gives his Shakespeare talk. Stephen senses that he can dazzle his audience with his knowledge of Shakespearean works, sources, criticism and biographies, an approach to authority well known to contemporary academics, and echoed in Joyce's critical works. Stephen tries to offer an ordered presentation; he entices his auditors with the promise of a succession of secrets, a mystery solved, a male origin at the centre. The mental debunking Stephen practises on each member of his audience creates an attitude of aloof superiority, derivable from priestly instructors like the teacher of 'An Encounter', or the romantic heroes he has found for himself. His discourse is thoroughly that of the male academic, and he has learned it well. At the close of *A Portrait* he considers himself a missionary, especially to the female members of his race. The early rejected pages of *Stephen Hero* had contained some aesthetic discussion between Stephen and his mother (*SH* 83-8). The only remnant in *A Portrait* is a religious discussion:

> 24 March: Began with a discussion with my mother. Subject: B.V.M. Handicapped by my sex and youth. To escape held up relations between Jesus and Papa against those between Mary and her son. Said religion was not a lying-in hospital. Mother indulgent. Said I have a queer mind and have read too much. Not true. Have read little and understood less. (*P* 248)

Stephen's humility is rare and privately expressed in a diary, interestingly a form more closely related to women than his public discourses of 'Scylla and Charybdis', 'Aeolus', and 'Oxen of the Sun'.

Finnegans Wake offers male historians and pedants as well as Stephen Dedalus' artistic equivalent, Shem the pen. Shem's brother, Shaun the post, is the political, institutional authority figure of the *Wake*, and as Jaun takes on the professorial role to a new constituency, the young women of St Bride's Academy. He offers a very limited canon to the women, one designed to enforce the patriarchal norm of female chastity:

> I'd burn the books that grieve you and light an allassundrian bompyre that would suffragate Tome Plyfire or Zolfanerole. Perousse instate your *Weekly Standerd,* our verile organ that is ethelred by all pressdom. (*FW* 439.34-440.1)

Jaun's book burning would eliminate the sufragette text and send Issy to a 'v[i]rile organ' connected with male institutions of kingship, the priesthood and the press. While Jaun is most obviously destroying the library at Alexandria, he also seems to burn Alexandra College, Dublin's first institution for women's higher education (founded 1866). In his role as postal deliverer, he is unreliable in delivering women's letters. Jaun's booklist deserves more extensive attention than I can give it here. It is heavy on Catholic chastity tracts. Two interesting items are 'Through Hill with the Papers (mostly boys) by the divine comic Centi Alligator'—which preserves Dante on the list, while casting sexual aspersions at the papacy—and Jaun's admission 'I used to follow Mary Liddlelambe's flitsy tales, especially with seentaminted sauce' (440.5-6, .18-19). Though Jaun stereotypically accused Mary Lamb of sentimentality, he also suggests the importance of *The Adventures of Ulysses*, which she co-authored, as an early resource for Joyce.

It becomes evident in the course of *Ulysses* that most of Dublin does not read the academically-approved, classical canon in which Stephen is educated. Bloom begins the day reading a prize story, 'Matcham's Masterstroke' in the penny weekly, *Titbits*, a paper Joyce's father enjoyed; Joyce submitted a story to it unsuccessfully. Bloom times his bowel movements to the reading, analysing the genre as he goes:

> Neat certainly. *Matcham often thinks of the masterstroke by which he won the laughing witch who now.* Begins and ends morally. *Hand in Hand.* Smart. He glanced back through what he had read and, while feeling his water flow quietly, he envied kindly Mr Beaufoy who had written and received payment of three pounds, thirteen and six. (4.513-17)

This story of male mastery reinforces patriarchal social arrangements, as Bloom realizes in spotting the moral beginning and end. The spirited female of detective fiction reappears in the 'laughing witch'. And it all is part of a clever financial arrangement, in which Bloom would like to share, claiming joint authorship with a story 'By Mr and Mrs L.M. Bloom'. The story he considers writing is about Molly and Blazes Boylan, her lover in the course of *Ulysses* (4.502-3, .513-30). With this materstroke, Joyce gives *Ulysses* a parallel in popular romance, to match the much celebrated classical parallel from Homer. We learn in the 'Calypso' episode that Molly has finished the novel *Ruby, Pride of the Ring*, and remarks 'nothing smutty in it. Is she in love with the first fellow all the time?' (4.355-6). Thus both she and Bloom are readers of romances. The exotics of smut and circus provide perhaps the sort of fantasy escape sought by contemporary readers of romances, as described in Radway's *Reading the Romance*. Bloom later obtains a new book for Molly, *The Sweets of Sin*, by Paul de Kock. Bloom also has the resources of the Capel Street Library, where, echoing the boy of 'An Encounter', he has borrowed something in the detective line, Conan Doyle's *The Stark-Munro Letters*.

The epigraph of this chapter calls attention to Bloom's own modest library and its disarray in the wake of Molly's cleaning efforts. This collection of 'inverted volumes improperly arranged' offers its own views of history, literature and women's use of books, but can only be discussed briefly here for its relation to the literary canon. It includes Lockhart's *Life of Napoleon* with 'marginal annotations, minimizing victories, aggrandizing defeats of the protagonist' (17.1381-2). The marginalia are an inheritance from Molly's father, Major Tweedy of the British Army, who has his own national angle on the conflicts. In effect though, this palimpsest deconstructs the military hero studied by young Stephen. A second historical work, *History of the Russo-Turkish War*, was probably also Tweedy's contribution, since it bears the label of a Gibralter library. A third volume of history would seem to be more to Bloom's taste, *The Secret History of the Court of Charles II*, since it offers potential romance and intrigue, rather than war history. There is also a novel by Irish nationalist William O'Brien, *When We were Boys*, which romanticizes the Fenian brotherhood. It should be considered male nationalist romance, a subject we return to in chapter 3.

Bloom's collection is hardly an example of triumphant mainstreaming. There is no literature by women. But 'literature' by men is hardly triumphant either. Bloom has only Shakespeare and two volumes of poetry by obscure Irishmen. His considerable collection of travel books, however, could be considered a feminine genre; they are also fitting to a modern day Odysseus. The books on maths and astron-

omy and the presence of a volume by Darwin would seem to
represent Bloom's rational, scientific, masculine aspect.
During the day, the books have become rearranged (mis-
arranged, according to Bloom) presumably by Molly as she
prepared for Boylan's visit. Bloom's verdict on 'the deficient
appreciation of literature possessed by females' works
several ways. Bloom feels superior as a guardian of literature. But we may well question his selection as literature.
Though Bloom doesn't intend it, his remarks also call into
question the access to literature women have been granted,
and ask why women should be expected to appreciate what
men have collected as literature, or the way that they have
arranged it.

Women writers are alluded to repeatedly in *Ulysses*, but
usually not in complimentary terms. Some fall victim to
Joyce's attitudes toward the movements with which they are
associated. Such is the case with Mme Helena Blavatsky,
one of the theoretical sources for the Dublin Theosophical
movement, and a woman now taken seriously by feminists
for her connection to 'ancient wisdom'.[18] Stephen mentally
debunks her in 'Scylla and Charybdis', both for her theos-
ophy and for her public posturings. He uses bawdy suggestions worthy of Buck Mulligan to trivialize her, 'Mrs
Cooper Oakley once glimpsed our very illustrious sister
H.P.B.'s elemental' (9.71). Joyce would find Blavatsky's
mysteries and especially her letters increasingly useful in
Finnegans Wake. Lady Gregory, a founder of the Irish
Literary Theatre, folklorist, playwright and patron of
Yeats, is given disrespectful treatment in 'Scylla and
Charybdis' in a text more definitely Mulligan's:

> —Longworth is awfully sick, he said, after what you wrote
> about that old hake Gregory. O you inquisitional drunken
> jewjesuit! She gets you a job on the paper and then you go and
> slate her drivel to Jaysus. Couldn't you do the Yeats touch?
> (9.1158-60)[19]

Mulligan suggests sexual liaison in Yeats' 'touch', and
also subjects Gregory to the abuses of age. His reproach
of Stephen for ingratitude, by echoing his remarks on

Stephen's mother in the 'Telemachus' episode, touches a sensitive nerve. References to Susan Mitchell, another important female member of the Irish revival, show that she is included and appreciated by the group: 'Did you hear Miss Mitchell's joke about Moore and Martyn? That Moore is Martyn's wild oats? Awfully clever, isn't it?' (9.306-8). Mitchell proved herself as capable of the Irish art of satire as men like George Moore, and here reinforces Stephen's mental disrespect for figures of the revival. She hints at homosexuality, as does Mulligan in his satires later in the chapter. 'Clever' is an epithet well short of 'brilliant' and one frequently used in faint praise of women. Unlike Stephen, however, Mitchell has the attention of the Dublin literati.

'Scylla and Charybdis' provides one of *Ulysses'* first examples of women writers of popular fiction in the allusion to *The Sorrows of Satan*, a novel by Marie Corelli:

—Have you found those six brave medicals, John Eglinton asked with elder's gall, to write *Paradise Lost* at your dictation? *The Sorrows of Satan* he calls it.
　　　Smile. Smile Cranly's smile.
　　　　First he tickled her
　　　　Then he patted her
　　　　Then he passed the female catheter (9.18-24)

By invoking Corelli's title for a project of rewriting Milton, Stephen mocks both authors. This achieves the larger aim of parodying Joyce's effort to rewrite Homer in *Ulysses*. Stephen must know of Corelli's work to use her book title, but he gives no thought to her as a writer. The medical rhyme quoted above undermines any sense of a woman's achievement, or even her physical autonomy. The allusion does bring attention to Joyce's practice of reading popular women's fiction. Maria Cummins' *The Lamplighter* is referred to repeatedly in *Ulysses*, and it is clear that both Gerty MacDowell and Molly Bloom enjoy a constant diet of heroines' texts, as does the sailor in the 'Eumaeus' episode, who had been reading *Red as a Rose is She* by Rhoda Broughton (16.1680). Corelli's novels feature heroines

who, like Corelli, might be authors or performers. They
are menaced by satanic heroes in melodramatic plots and
sexual intrigues, but brought back to hegemonic propriety
through generous doses of religious sermonizing. Corelli
offers a blend of the mysticism and pseudo-science of her
era, making her romances fascinating social texts. There are
special reasons for placing an allusion to Corelli in the
'Scylla and Charybdis' chapter. Like Stephen, Corelli
identified with Shakespeare, alluding to him incessantly in
her works. She even took up permanent residence in
Stratford-upon-Avon. Unlike Stephen, Corelli was a successful author with sensitivity to the demands of her readership; even her slight presence works ironically against
Stephen's aloof discourse, and prepares the way for the
more common textual sources increasingly evident in later
Joyce. Adaline Glasheen has caught an allusion to Corelli in
the 'Mime' chapter of *Finnegans Wake* (II.I) where she
senses Joyce's borrowing of Corelli's moral/sexual blend.[20]

Joyce never embraced the techniques of the best-known
women novelists of the nineteenth century, Jane Austen,
the Brontës and George Eliot, though he does allude to
Eliot's *The Mill on the Floss* (*FW* 213.2) and Emily Brontë's
Wuthering Heights (*FW* 229.3-4, 241.6) in the 'Anna Livia'
chapter (I.8) of *Finnegans Wake*. ALP, the central figure
of this chapter, also bestows the writing of two Irish women
writers, Speranza Wilde and Emily Lawless, upon the
world as gifts (210.33, 211.24). Gender aside, the forms of
nineteenth-century fiction were generally unsuited to the
modernist novel of Woolf, as well as Joyce. Woolf hailed
Brontë, Eliot and especially Austen, but acknowledged that
in the writing of the Georgians (who included herself as well
as Joyce), 'the accent falls differently from of old'.[21] Joyce
realized the popular importance of romance—fiction by and
about women—as we have noted through Bloom's canon.
But he does not write heroines' texts, as they have been
defined in recent feminist narrative theory. Joyce's central
protagonist is almost always male, though there are clear
heroines' sub-texts, as we have noted with Ann Hathaway
and will examine in later chapters. Joyce's narrative never

culminates in marriage. Stephen never gets that far. Joyce's more mature men and women in 'The Dead', *Exiles, Ulysses* and *Finnegans Wake* have moved on to new concerns. Though it trades on the heroine's text, 'The Mime' chapter of the *Wake* denies the romantic ending in marriage or death of the heroine.

Joyce did work inside other women's genres. The diary at the end of *A Portrait* offered an important stylistic shift. Women's letters come into their own in *Finnegans Wake*, particularly in the 'mamafesta' of chapter I.5. The text offers several versions of a lost letter or several lost letters, likely written by women. One letter is from Boston, Mass., by a young girl, probably Issy, the daughter figure of the *Wake*. It bears family news, comments on the weather, serves as thank-you note, and focuses upon important men, 'the *lovely* face of some born gentleman', and the 'grand funferall of poor Father Michael' (111.8-20). A second document seems to come from ALP in the role of a hen. It attempts to clear the father, HCE, by telling 'the cock's trootabout him' though its revelations about his efforts 'to see life foully' may only make him seem more questionable (113.12-13).

The text(s) of the mamafesta and the signature(s) of the author(s) have been disfigured, and pedantic discussions of the authoritative methods for attribution and interpretation compete with and very nearly displace the female texts. Joyce seems to be offering a critique of the historical treatment of women's writing by the male academic establishment. One text of the mamafesta vigorously promotes the woman writer. A female scholar is encouraged to respond to the male interpreters: 'Gee up, girly! The quad gospellers may own the targum but any othe the Zingari scoolerim may pick a peck of kindlings yet from the sack of auld hensyne.' What she offers comes closer to being a feminist manifesto than the two letters just referred to, but it blends feminist authority into maternity. Her interpretation is strewn with male theory—biology as destiny, Newman, and Kipling's 'white burden'. Yet she also hopes for feminist utopias and debunks the male 'gloompourers' who would

deny woman's place as writer. In her literary history, the
woman writer offers an oasis, perhaps the female modernist
alternative to T.S. Eliot's 'The Wasteland':

> Lead, kindly fowl! They always did: ask the ages. What bird
> has done yesterday man may do next year, be it fly, be it moult,
> be it hatch, be it agreement in the nest. For her socioscientific
> sense is sound as a bell, sir, her volucrine automutativeness
> right on normalcy: she knows, she just feels she was kind of
> born to lay and love eggs (trust her to propagate the species and
> hoosh her fluffballs safe through din and danger!); lastly but
> mostly, in her genesic field it is all game and no gammon; she is
> ladylike in everything she does and plays the gentleman's part
> every time. Let us auspice it! Yes, before all this has time to
> end the golden age must return with its vengeance. Man will
> become dirigible, Ague will be rejuvenated, woman with her
> ridiculous white burden will breach by one step sublime incu-
> bation, the manewanting human lioness with her dishorned
> discipular manram will lie down together publicly flank upon
> fleece. No, assuredly, they are not justified, those gloom-
> pourers who grouse that letters have never been quite their old
> selves again since that weird weekday in bleak Janiveer (yet
> how palmy date in a waste's oasis!) when to the shock of both,
> Biddy Doran looked at literature. (112.9-28)

From the start of *Finnegans Wake*, the hen takes possession of history. After the battle between Wellington and
Napoleon, she takes to the 'bleakbardfields' (10.34) and
begins 'picking here, pecking there, pussypussy plunder-
pussy' (11.12-13). 'How bootifull and how truetowife of
her, when strengly forebidden, to steal our historic presents
from the past postpropheticals so as to will make us all
lordly heirs and ladymaidesses of a pretty nice kettle of
fruit' (11.29-32). She gives no particular prominence to
ancient Greek patriarchal history, 'Hou! Hou! Gricks may
rise and Troysirs full (there being two sights for ever a
picture) for in the byways of a high improvidence that's
what makes life work leaving.... Let young wimmun run
away with the story and let young men talk smooth behind
the buttelar's back' (11.35-12.4).
In chapter I.8, washerwomen rewrite the history of

HCE, using his dirty linen as their source of information, and recentring upon the history of ALP, who has complained '*By earth and the coludy but I badly want a brand-new bankside, bedamp and I do, and a plumper at that!* (200.6-12; 201.5-20). ALP has been unable to find 'whuon the annals her gaveller was' (202.23-4), suggesting the inadequacy of male historians. The washerwomen are sensitive to the problems of lost women's history: 'And one of Biddy's beads went bobbing till she rounded up lost hister-eve with a marigold and a cobbler's candle in a side strain of a main drain of a manzinahurries off Bachelor's Walk' (213.36-214.3).[22] Men in a hurry, and bachelors have marginalized women, lost the story of Eve, and knowledge of 'hister', the womb, hysteria. Women are left with what instruments they can scavenge—a marigold or a candle—to recover their past.

Likewise, Kate, janatrix of the 'Willingdone Museyroom', reinterprets history, cataloguing the armaments of war in a way that renders them absurd. She includes the 'jinnies' and their 'handmade's book of stralegy' in her account (8.32-4). Female 'stralegy' is not entirely affirmative. The jinnies sent HCE diverting dispatches and consort with his male enemies.[23] ALP distributes some gifts of trouble to those who have disparaged HCE, imitating the the act of an angered God at the fall in *Genesis*, as well as Demeter. The Prankquean is capable of comparable protest (kidnapping the children of Jarl van Hoother), on her own behalf. But, as ALP's catalogue of potential titles for her letter suggests, her collection is the basis of *Finnegans Wake* (104.6-107.7). Its paradigm is no longer the classical text, but comes much closer to the 'litters' of obscure, collective, working-class and even non-human origin, recovered and even written by the hen and her sisters.

CHAPTER THREE

Gender, Discourse and Culture

Did you note that worrid expressionism on his megalogue? A
full octavium below me! And did you hear his browrings rattle-
making when he was preaching to himself? And, whoa! do you
twig the schamlooking leaf greeping ghastly down his blousy-
frock? Our national umbloom! Areesh! (*FW* 467.7-11)

James Joyce has been widely praised for re-creating a
bourgeois, barely post-Victorian Dublin world in the words
of *Dubliners, A Portrait* and *Ulysses*. As is appropriate to
his original model, Joyce distributes men and women to
largely separate, but occasionally overlapping territories. If
we apply the anthropological feminist model of overlapping
circles of male and female sub-cultures, we find in Joyce a
particularly rich recording of the discourse and experience
of all-male culture. We visit the male preserves of boys'
schools, pubs, political committee rooms, a businessmen's
retreat, a funeral, the inner sanctum of a library, a newspaper office, and a medical students' lounge in a hospital. In
sections of the *Dubliners* stories and *A Portrait*, and at the
beginning and end of Leopold Bloom's day in *Ulysses*, men
enter a domestic realm shared with women. But even in
many scenes where women are present, as in the formal
dinner scenes of 'The Dead' and *A Portrait*, men interact
mainly with one another or are lost in their own performance and/or thoughts. Family scenes tend to be presided
over by a man. His rhetoric is appropriate to a position of
patriarchal power, even though that power may already be

46

undermined. Joyce's less known drama, *Exiles*, has a domestic setting shared by men and women. But, as we shall see, it offers a meaningful variant from Dublin culture. As noted in chapter 2, Joyce rarely supplies a female perspective or visits an all-female territory (see *J & F*, 133-7). Gerty MacDowell will allow us to investigate the discourse of romance available in Dublin women's culture, through her mental reactions to her girlfriends and Leopold Bloom. I reserve a discussion of female language and narrative, to the extent that Joyce treats them, for chapter 5. Michel Foucault, defines 'discursive practice' as 'a body of anonymous, historical rules, always determined in the time and space that have defined a given period, and for a given social, economic, geographical, or linguistic area, the conditions of operation of the enunciative function'.[1] I add to this the sense that gender profoundly conditions discourse. The colonial status of the Irish is also of importance. As was the case in chapter 2, this chapter focuses upon human experience in the conscious range as realistically represented. For theory, it makes use of Lacanian cultural paradigms, Marxist concepts of economy and power, feminist research on narrative, and feminist critique of sex roles.

In chapter 2, while examining issues of canonical history and literature, we charted Stephen Dedalus' acquisition of academic male discourse from the classical and theological education provided by the Jesuits. I shall begin this chapter by discussing a second male discourse taught to Stephen by his father, Simon. It is bourgeois Irish nationalist discourse and it prepares Stephen's way with the men of Dublin. Leopold Bloom is often hailed as the 'womanly man', yet he respects the authority of Stephen's academic discourse, and is uncritical of Simon Dedalus' performances. Bloom can enunciate another form of male discourse, the scientific, and does so throughout *Ulysses*. Though tempting, a gender-sensitive investigation of the scientific in Joyce must await another study.

Simon Dedalus offers his son's first rhetorical model in the story-telling at the opening of *A Portrait of the Artist as a Young Man*. Lacanian theory associates the paternal phallus with the *logos* or word, as well as the laws by which society operates, hence the importance of this narration in supplying Stephen with the rules of discourse. By making 'Baby Tuckoo' or Stephen the subject or centre of his narrative, Simon encourages the self-centred, egotistical, solipsistic narrative so obvious throughout Stephen's artistic development. The early story-telling is one in a series of vignettes where Stephen witnesses a performance, a personal or political discourse by his father, and is moved to sort out his own personal history and eventually his artistic course. Mrs Dedalus, on the other hand, has had most of her performances edited out of *A Portrait*. Dialogues are recalled, not recorded at length. She complies generally with the stereotypically feminine roles of accompanist and observer, displaying a muted and inhibited discourse, or providing a mouthpiece for the words of the father or the patriarchal church.[2] We see her teamed with Stephen's Aunt 'Dante', but never in exclusively female company.

Simon's major performances include the Christmas dinner scene, where he is patriarchal host—wielder of the knife, dispenser of the sauce, and instigator of the political discussion that divides the family along gender lines and sunders Stephen's sense of a moral world order. Simon is again on stage in Cork (*P* 188ff.), where he sentimentally recalls his personal past, including his prowess with women and his attachment to his father. In another scene, Simon makes a political speech outside the former Irish House of Commons, regretting the diminishment of public men (96-7). Scattered through *A Portrait* are his pearls of paternal wisdom. To facilitate Stephen's male-bonding at school, Simon advises 'never to peach on a fellow' (9). Simon's discourses have their antecedents in *Dubliners* in the speech of Joe Hynes in 'Ivy Day in the Committee Room' and the banquet address of Gabriel Conroy in 'The Dead'. Simon says less in *Ulysses*, but he moves about the male preserves of the city, and everywhere he is or has been, we find recollections and repetitions of his discourse. Significantly, so does Stephen. The rhetorical tropes of the headlines printed in 'Aeolus' are related to his discourse. Simon's sort of talk culminates in the 'Cyclops' chapter of *Ulysses* but echoes still in the *Finnegans Wake* speeches of the four chroniclers and Shaun as 'Jaun the Boast' (*FW* 469.29) with his 'barrel of leaking rhetoric' (*FW* 429.8), 'stone of law' (430.6), and the epigraph used for this chapter. Hugh Kenner describes the spectacle of a man speaking in public as 'a paradigmatic communal act, offering to make sense of what he and his listeners confront together'. He suggests that Dublin men simply lack the sense of history needed to carry off more than 'pieces of inappropriate virtuosity' or 'Pyrrhonism in the pub'.[3] I suggest that their failures lead us on to deconstruct the male speech act itself, and to recover alternate acts and conceptions of community more inclusive of women, and less characterized by forced unities.

Even though his economic prowess steadily declines in *A Portrait*, Simon clings to a rhetoric of masterful command. When he can no longer afford to send Stephen to prestigious Clongowes Wood College, Simon takes pride in having arranged with Father Conmee for Stephen's place in the local Jesuit school, Belvedere. His self-satisfaction comes from a sense of knowing and manipulating a system and implies complicity in social and intellectual hierarchies and male networks. He performs for the family, with Mrs Dedalus as his assistant. The narrator implies criticism, with references to his busy tongue and calculations of Simon's repetitions:

> One evening his father came home full of news which kept his tongue busy all through dinner . . . .
> —I walked bang into him, said Mr Dedalus for the fourth time, just at the corner of the square.
> —Then I suppose, said Mrs Dedalus, he will be able to arrange it. I mean about Belvedere.
> —Of course he will, said Mr Dedalus. Don't I tell you he's provincial of the order now?
> —I never liked the idea of sending him to the christian brothers myself, said Mrs Dedalus.
> —Christian brothers be damned! said Mr Dedalus. Is it with Paddy Stink and Mickey Mud? No, let him stick to the

jesuits in God's name since he began with them. They'll be of
service to him in after years. Those are the fellows that can get
you a position. (71)

The most extensive, varied, virtuoso performance by
Simon is the earlier Christmas dinner scene, which also
marks an epoch in Stephen's cultural passage into man-
hood. Stephen has survived the anxieties of the young male
world at Clongowes and is fulfilling a dreamed-of return
home. Triumphal return to the family from the larger,
public world of Clongowes was a male pattern and freedom
in that era. The Dedalus' educational priorities are reminiscent of 'Arthur's education fund' in Virginia Woolf's
Three Guineas. Stephen also takes on the privileges of an
adult occasion and an Eton suit, a uniform of social prestige,
notably of British public school design. Simon's tears at
seeing the suit betray a male identification, Simon thinking
back to his father (30). Stephen recalls the suit years later,
and Leopold Bloom has a vision of his long-dead son in
similar garb in *Ulysses*.

The argument which develops at Christmas dinner is
strongly marked by gender. Simon has been out walking
with his radical nationalist friend Mr Casey. The Sunday or
holiday walk is another male institution. Politics is a usual
topic, and a suburban pub is a probable destination, since
drinking laws limited serving to bona-fide travellers.
Stephen joins his father and Uncle Charles on their consti-
tutionals. He listens and thinks that he is finding a future
for himself.

> Trudging along the road or standing in some grimy wayside
> publichouse his elders spoke constantly of the subjects nearer
> their hearts, of Irish politics, of Munster and of the legends of
> their own family, to all of which Stephen lent an avid ear. . . .
> The hour when he too would take part in the life of that world
> seemed drawing near and in secret he began to make ready for
> the great part which he felt awaited him.(62)

Simon Dedalus comes to Christmas dinner prepared by
discussion with a like-minded Parnellite to vindicate his

fallen political hero. In this territory of mixed gender, Simon meets opposition in Mrs Riordan (Dante), whom Stephen takes as a figure of some intellectual and moral authority, but already sees as subordinate to males and a disappointment in life. He assumes she knows less than priests and recalls his father's assessment of her as a 'spoiled nun' (35). Stephen is clearly more interested in Mr Casey, an exotic from a sphere of male action and violence, while Dante is a regular domestic feature. Stephen imagines Casey's bold adventures and dangerous connections through the half-told recollections cherished by his father. He likes to sit by Casey and looks 'with affection' at his face, which has the same 'fierce' appeal that attracted the boy of 'An Encounter' to the exotic female figures of detective fiction (35). Thus Stephen enters the dinner scene with a male bias. At the end, when Dante storms out consoled and accompanied by Mrs Dedalus, Stephen is fixed with the men.

Simon Dedalus has an array of rhetorical devices. Cryptic allusions to tales shared with Mr Casey give them mysterious attractiveness and exclude Dante. Simon's first remark to her accentuates their different worlds:

—You didn't stir out at all, Mrs Riordan?
Dante frowned and said shortly:
—No. (28)

Dante's curtness suggests pre-existing difficulties; perhaps she anticipates the baiting techniques that regularly appear in Simon's apparently jovial discourse. Simon does arouse her finally with an anti-clerical recollection to the appreciative Mr Casey. Simon admires a 'good answer' made to a canon who had spoken of politics from the pulpit. Dante is alone in her defence of the role of the church, though Mrs Dedalus seems a sympathizer, silenced by her husband's domination. Dante comes across as a defender of strict moral priorities. Her thinking and even her rhetoric derive from church fathers, not from any female culture. The defence, once summoned, is relentless and ends in the apocalyptic, vengeful discourse of a hell-fire sermon: 'Devil

out of hell! We won! We crushed him to death!' It is
impossible to idealize this discourse or identify it as a feminist alternative to Simon's. Its product is sex war.

Simon's speech is far more amusing than Dante's and his
tearful breakdown at the end of the scene tends to evoke the
reader's sympathy. His discourse is just as sinister as
Dante's, however. We have seen two examples of baiting.
There are others, calling the turkey's tail 'the pope's nose',
and a reference to 'strangers' in the neighbourhood (foreign
intruders, to an Irish audience) (32-33). Simon moves on to
ad hominem invective against priests: 'Respect! he said. Is
it for Billy with the lip or for the tub of guts up in Armagh?
Respect!' Simon adds the dimension of physical mimicry, 'a
grimace of heavy bestiality and . . . a lapping noise with his
lips' (33). In the late parts of his performance, Simon
receives his friend's support, Mr Casey providing useful
nods and reinforcing echoes of Simon's opinions. To Dante's
charge of 'renegade' Catholicism, Casey embraces a significantly male-identified Catholicism: 'I am a catholic as my
father was and his father before him . . . ' (34). Indeed,
Catholicism does have different male and female versions in
Ireland, Joyce suggests repeatedly.

Casey's own narrative performance is the story of 'the
famous spit'. Casey creates himself as the hero at the centre
of his narrative. As in the larger Christmas dinner scene,
there is female opposition, an old woman, who like Dante
lacks the wit so apparent in the men. Casey prepares his
response, holding off through several of her verbal assaults,
the delay in the narrative arousing the curiosity of his audience and Simon's appreciative prompting. The woman
plays right into his hands, presenting her face for his *'Phth!'*,
which Casey delivers twice, for effect, in his narrative. Like
Simon, he also has skills of mimicry, which he turns toward
the representation of her screams and exclamations (37).
Casey's spit offers paradigms of male physical and sexual
assault upon a woman grown despicable by age as well as
speech. Male production denies female speech. The old
woman's message, a condemnation of Parnell's extramarital
love, Kitty O'Shea, shows complicity in the moral norms of

male hegemony, a familiar aspect of woman's consciousness in the shared culture, to which Joyce was sensitive.

Simon's final subject at Christmas dinner, the fall of the great man of Irish history, Charles Stuart Parnell, is related to our discussion of history in chapter 2. Simon's version of Irish history is peopled by great and infamous men, and treats of a series of wars and political struggles, much like the Roman history studied by young Stephen or the contents of the Museyroom in *Finnegans Wake*. In Ireland, as Kenner notes, defeat and betrayal are recurrent outcomes, and the discourse takes on tones of regret and nostalgia for bygone greatness. Simon's lists of former heroes and gross betrayers are long and embellished, the heroes including his male ancestors. He began his Christmas remarks with a gesture toward the portrait of his grandfather, 'condemned to death as a whiteboy' (38). In Cork, Simon reminisces tearfully about his father. In the street by the old House of Commons, he recalls Flood, Grattan and other parliamentarians predating the Act of Union (a parliamentary unification of Ireland with England which occurred in 1800). Simon follows his citation of the heroic grandfather with a well-prepared list of traitor priests:

> —Didn't the bishops of Ireland betray us in the time of the union when bishop Lanigan presented an address of loyalty to the Marquess Cornwallis? Didn't the bishops and priests sell the aspirations of their country in 1829 in return for catholic emancipation? Didn't they denounce the fenian movement from the pulpit and the confessionbox? And didn't they dishonour the ashes of Terence Bellew MacManus? (38)

Simon's final tearful utterances on Parnell are familiar to readers of 'Ivy Day in the Committee Room', where Joe Hynes shares both the subject and the discourse, as he will again on the all-male occasion of the funeral in the 'Hades' chapter of *Ulysses*. Stephen's memories of Paris in the 'Proteus' episode of *Ulysses* are haunted by a fallen Fenian father, Kevin Egan.

Comparable display of historical recall is evident also in the 'Aeolus' episode of *Ulysses*, where the great journalist

Ignatius Gallaher, is lionized for his communication of details of the Phoenix Park murders, and where great Irish orators are memorialized. Readers can experience bravado more directly from Gallaher in the central pub scene of the *Dubliners* story, 'A Little Cloud' or from Buck Mulligan in the opening episode of *Ulysses*. Additional examples of Irish national discourse are provided by the keeper of the cab shelter, the sailor and Leopold Bloom in the 'Eumaeus' episode of *Ulysses* and, on the unionist side, by Mr Deasy in 'Nestor'. The preaching of HCE in *Finnegans Wake* receives more open mockery from his sons than Stephen's implied disappointment in Simon. As Joyce's final male rhetorician, HCE develops a stammer that matches his daughter's lisp (*FW* 197.6, 467.9).

The outstanding example is the 'Cyclops' episode, where the cantankerous narrator, the 'citizen', Joe Hynes and Bloom all participate; they compete to present versions of Irish history of varying nationalist intensity. The setting is exclusively male, Barney Kiernan's pub, a tavern of little distinction, judging by the patrons' behaviour and the presence of the mangy dog, Garryowen. The narrator is a collector of debts, a public role resembling the limited employment of Joyce's own father, and making him a stand-in for Simon Dedalus. The narrator is a master of invective from the moment he offers the 'weight of his tongue' to a 'bloody' sweep who bumps into him at the start of the chapter. The objects of his invective include the participants in the pub discussions, and even their rhetorical styles. No one is more harshly treated by him than Bloom. The narrator adds Pisser Burke's reports on Bloom as a debater at Barney Kiernan's:

And the citizen and Bloom having an argument about the point, the brothers Sheares and Wolfe Tone beyond on Arbour Hill and Robert Emmet and die for your country, the Tommy Moore touch about Sara Curran and she's far from the land. And Bloom, of course, with his knockmedown cigar putting on swank with his lardy face. Phenomenon! . . . Jesus, I had to laugh at pisser Burke taking them off chewing the fat. And Bloom with his *but don't you see?* and *but on the other hand*. And sure, more be token . . . Phenomenon! (*U* 12.498-518)

Epic Irish heroism has a new dimension and receives a humorous, parodic treatment in interpolated lists and narratives throughout the chapter. The lists are undermined by their frequency, exaggerated length and the insertion of unlikely entries. Humour and improbability are achieved by the occasional citation of a female name. The epicized citizen wears seastones hanging from his girdle 'graven with rude yet striking art the tribal images of many Irish heroes and heroines of antiquity'. The list begins predictably enough with Cuchulin, Conn of hundred battles, and Niall of nine hostages, but moves on to the actress Peg Woffington, the Mother of the Maccabees, 'The Woman Who Didn't', Cleopatra and Lady Godiva (12.174-99). Interestingly, the most heroic of the women from Irish myth, Maeve, is omitted. The narrator is unsympathetic in his report of the patriotic discourses of both the citizen and Hynes:

> So of course the citizen was only waiting for the wink of the word and he starts gassing out of him about the invincibles and the old guard and the men of sixtyseven and who fears to speak of ninetyeight and Joe with him about all the fellows that were hanged, drawn and transported for the cause by drumhead courtmartial and a new Ireland and new this, that and the other. (12.479-84)

Examples of the nostalgic male regretting his losses are numerous in Joyce, as are his devices for defamiliarizing (distancing) us from their performances. Gabriel Conroy displays the same tendency, though his subject is lost singers and the more expansive hospitality that preceded the age he characterizes as 'hypereducated' (203). This criticism is hypocritical if applied to himself; vindictive and ineffectual if aimed at the departed Miss Ivors. In 'Cyclops', a drunken Bob Doran weeps for the sake of weeping over Paddy Dignam's death, though unable to get the deceased man's name correct (12.388-403). Joyce makes his most direct statement on mournful history in two essays of 1902 and 1903, both about the nineteenth-century Irish nationalist poet, James Clarence Mangan. He identifies the 'high

traditions of Mangan's race' as 'love of sorrow for the sake of
sorrow and despair and fearful menaces' (*CW* 82). He
regrets Mangan's cries 'against the injustice of despoilers' as
'the latest and worst part of a legend upon which the line
has never been drawn out and which divides against itself as
it moves down the cycles' (*CW* 81-2; reiterated 185). It is a
tradition that an 'eager spirit' would 'cast down', not imitate
or canonize. Hélène Cixous, in discussing the castration
complex as a male myth, identifies mourning over loss as a
distinctly male activity, a feminist interpretation with
obvious relevance to Simon's role in Stephen's supposed
castration complex and Simon's own mourning.[4]

Simon Dedalus' discourse in *A Portrait* gets less and less
attention and sympathy as Stephen matures. By the time
they travel to Cork, Simon's speeches to Stephen have no
audience:

> Stephen watched the three glasses being raised from the
> counter as his father and his two cronies drank to the memory
> of their past. An abyss of fortune or of temperament sundered
> him from them. His mind seemed older than theirs: and it shone
> coldly on their strifes and happiness and regrets like a moon
> upon a younger earth. No life or youth stirred in him as it had
> stirred in them. He had known neither the pleasure of com-
> panionship with others nor the vigour of rude male health nor
> filial piety. . . . he was drifting amid life like the barren shell of
> the moon. (*P* 95-6)

Stephen has lost his personal past and rejected his national
past and the usual male bonds, turning again to Shelley and
to an icy, lunar brooding, the moon connecting him with
a usual female symbol. As Maud Ellmann points out,
Stephen is unable to find the name of his father engraved in
his old schoolroom in Cork.[5] He finds, instead, the word
'foetus' which profoundly upsets his sense of phallic masculine economy and order.

The identification of law with the father figure, as suggested in Lacanian psychoanalytic theory, is detectable
throughout 'Cyclops', where there are constant references
to lawsuits, courts and hangmen as well as abundant samples

of legal language. A profound historical identification between original Irish brehon law and the male heads of tribes
is made in one of the epic interruptions:

> And to the solemn court of Green street there came sir Frederick
> the Falconer. And he sat him there about the hour of five
> o'clock to administer the law of the brehons at the commission
> for all that and those parts to be holden in and for the county of
> the city of Dublin. And there sat with him the high sinhedrim
> of the twelve tribes of Iar, for every tribe one man, of the tribe
> of Patrick and of the tribe of Hugh and of the tribe of Owen and
> of the tribe of Conn and of the tribe of Oscar and of the tribe of
> Fergus and of the tribe of Finn. . . . (12.1120-8)

Although he bemoans and berates the conquest of Ireland,
the citizen embraces the tactics of force, kicking his dog,
predicting revenge on Ireland's enemies, glorifying violent
Gaelic sports as a tradition significantly dating back to the
Greeks and Romans (12.900), and finally hurling his biscuit
tin at Bloom, the effeminate, Jewish advocate of love over
'force, hatred, history, all that' (12.1481-5). 'Force' was the
title of an essay Joyce wrote at sixteen. The surviving pages
suggest that he acknowledged its pervasiveness as a human
principle. Conquest and subjection of one race over another,
Joyce identified specifically with 'the white man' (*CW* 20).
Young Joyce ends by advocating the use of force only for
'the brood of men now, in towns and cities' to subjugate
dubious personal qualities. Among the qualities to be overcome are 'the hurting word, the worthless taunt', deeds that
describe much of the hateful discourse of 'Cyclops'.

Women have a subsidiary or negative role in the male
historical discourse initiated by Simon Dedalus and sustained by figures like Mr Deasy and the citizen in 'Cyclops'.
The speakers of 'Cyclops' see women as adjuncts to men or
history; they are Robert Emmet's beloved or the English
King's mistress. As victims of rape or slaughter, women
help to build the citizen's case against oppressors of Ireland,
but no effort is made to establish the women's perspectives
(12.1507-10). Women are also represented as betrayers of
their lovers and husbands. The narrator defames Polly

Mooney Doran and Molly Bloom; the Irish epic text makes
a traitor of a Sara Curran figure, who quickly moves from
the condemned Robert Emmet to 'a handsome young Oxford
graduate' bearing 'an expensive engagement ring with
emeralds set in the form of a fourleaved shamrock' (12.667-
8). The citizen's list of betrayers starts with 'the adulteress and her paramour brought the Saxon robbers here'
(12.1157), a mistelling of the legend of Devorghilla, and
a typical scapegoating of woman. Other women like Mrs
Breen or even the Widow Dignam are potential objects for
infidelity, even to Bloom. As Stephen and Bloom walk off
into the night at the end of 'Eumaeus', the discussion includes 'sirens, enemies of man's reason, mingled with a
number of other topics of the same category, usurpers,
historical cases of the kind . . . ' (16.1889-91).

'Cyclops' offers equally severe defamation of any man
suspected of lacking virility. Bloom is the central suspect
and the narrator fantasizes him in a female domestic's cos-
tume: 'Gob, he'd adorn a sweeping brush, so he would, if
he only had a nurse's apron on him' (12.1477-8). Interestingly, Bloom remains on the periphery of the discourse of
'Cyclops', incapable of the same rhetoric. He has also been
marginal to Christian male discourse in the 'Hades' episode,
and removes himself from the rough-mannered clientele of
Burton's pub in 'Lestrygonians'. Bloom is eminently interruptable, a conversational fate which studies show to be
more commonly experienced by women.[6] The 'phallopyro-
technic designs' of Bloom's fantasy speeches in 'Circe' (U
15.1495) are interrupted periodically by persecutions,
problems as a speaker that persist for HCE. We have noted
the narrator's impatience with Bloom's rhetoric, but it is
possible that the narrator exaggerates Bloom's performance
(see 12.888-96). In more direct samples, Bloom's discourse
seems far more modest and understated than the citizen's or
even Joe Hynes'.

Leopold Bloom has participated in Irish political history.
Molly recalls with distaste his past political rhetoric. He was
a Parnellite. In 'Eumaeus', he recalls several times his
returning of Parnell's hat. It is hardly an event preserved in

history, or remarkable to traditional historians. To Bloom, Parnell's simple 'thank you' has merit; it substitutes for other forms of more militant and haughty greatness. Bloom fails in the political discourse at Barney Kiernan's pub. At his worst, he is pressured into chauvinistically declaiming a list of great Jewish men. Recalling his retort, that Jesus' father was a Jew, Bloom is still congratulating himself hours later, indicating that he aspires to male repartee. Bloom commands only fleeting authority as a speaker in 'Circe', where academic titles and arguments are mocked in quick succession, one author bearing the title, 'nationalgymnasiummuseumsanatoriumandsuspensoriumsordinaryprivatdocentgeneralhistoryspecialprofessordoctor', while 'delegates without exception expressed themselves in the strongest possible heterogeneous terms concerning the nameless barbarity which they had been called upon to witness' (12.567-71). Bloom's much considered message of love over hatred is something that the men of the pub cannot respond to, though its humanism has won Bloom the approval of a large segment of Joyce's readership, including Marilyn French.[7] Bloom seems more interested than other Dublin men in women's lives. Although his collection of female data is random and sketchy, and sometimes involves chauvinistic judgements, he is genuinely curious about women's experience; he checks on how a birth is progressing, takes notes on Molly's expressions, and in 'Circe' fantasizes life from a woman's perspective.

Exclusively female domains are rarely observed in Joyce. Stephen is as curious about them as Bloom. He imagines the rooms to which Emma Clery and her fellow female students retreat, and their 'quiet rosary of hours'. Bloom has positive thoughts about young women together, but not about nuns:

Girl friends at school, arms round each other's necks or with ten fingers locked, kissing and whispering secrets about nothing in the convent garden. Nuns with whitewashed faces, cool coifs and tier rosaries going up and down, vindictive too for what they can't get. Barbed wire. Be sure now and write to me.

And I'll write to you. Now won't you? Molly and Josie Powell.
Till Mr Right comes along, then meet once in a blue moon.

After the male alliance, Bloom imagines mutual antagonism
'picking holes in each other's appearance. . . . Wouldn't lend
each other a pinch of salt' (13.809-20). Women have re-
treated to the church in 'Araby', 'An Encounter', 'Counterparts', *A Portrait* and *Ulysses*, but the reader only goes to
church in male company, as in 'Grace', with Stephen or
with Bloom, and there the male rhetoric of the priest is on
display. The church typically offers women male-supervised
space and spirituality. Stephen finds a male rival in the
priest acting as confessor to Emma or even his own mother.
   Joyce does capture women's work with peripheral vision.
His scrupulous re-creation of turn-of-the-century Dublin
provides glimpses, sounds and sharp clear memories of
working-class women—a fishmonger in *Exiles*, a flower-
seller proclaiming herself Stephen's 'own girl' in *A Portrait*,
the servant girl beating a rug under Bloom's gaze in *Ulysses*,
and typists, one with spare time to correspond with Bloom,
others clearly doing better than Farrington in 'Counterparts'.
Women in stores sell to Maria of 'Clay', Little Chandler of
'A Little Cloud', to Blazes Boylan and Molly Bloom in
Ulysses. There are representatives of the 'oldest profession'
too. It is difficult to speak of the discourse of these women,
since their messages are often exclusively visual, and it is
difficult to know whether they are deliberate. If quoted at
all, they are heard briefly. They seem to be best remembered when they make a quick bid for attention or a pert
remark.
   Joyce works more extensively with middle-class women
seen, not in work outside the home, but in domestic roles:
in marriages, as mothers, or as single women visiting or
entertaining a group composed at least partly of family
members. Joyce's female domesticity represents middle-
class Catholic-Irish-Victorian norms. There are domestic
scenes in *Dubliners*; 'Counterparts', 'A Little Cloud', and
'Grace' shift the scene dramatically from male centres of
activity to a home setting where the female is a force. Joyce

uses the same tactic in *A Portrait* and *Ulysses* where a scene change to the Dedalus household serves to contrast Stephen's creative flights with the grim domestic situation supervised first by his mother in *A Portrait* and later by Dilly in *Ulysses*. In 'Araby' the boy's aunt sets food on the table and manages her nephew's needs while attending to her drunken husband and his friend. We meet Eveline musing at home, but learn about her work. She does the house-keeping, cares for younger siblings and also works in the public realm of the stores. The story denies her marriage and the fulfilment of a romantic plot. Annie Chandler is set amid the material goods of a recent middle-class marriage, which has failed to provide a romantic culmination. In 'The Dead' we meet the celibate Morkan sisters and their niece at their annual party, an event that provides a showcase for their profession of teaching music, work carried on largely at home. Mrs Mooney certainly acts powerfully in her own space, which is both familial and professional in 'The Boarding House'. Emma Clery aspires to education and the vote, issues covered directly in *Stephen Hero* though only suggested in *A Portrait* (*J & F,* 40-5, 135-9). Miss Ivors of 'The Dead' is a full-fledged professional woman, a teacher like Gabriel. She is an advocate of the public cause of Irish nationalism and goes on her own travels at night and to the west of Ireland, all ventures and territories not usually open to Dublin women, especially ones of the older generation. Molly Ivors troubles Gabriel with her ideas, and departs early, perhaps so as not to disturb the party. Gabriel finds comfort in the older Dublin generation and his supposedly simpler wife, the stay-at-home Gretta. But he soon learns that Gretta has a world of emotional experience that he has not traversed. It is an unconscious territory that interests Joyce as a mature writer far more than women's work or her tentative entries into the cultural discourse and territory formerly shaped and dominated by men.

Joyce's realism wears away particularly early with women, perhaps because they had always functioned for him as symbols and in myth, the latter a subject we will return to in chapter 4. The very believable old servant in *Exiles*,

Brigid, has the name of an Irish goddess and saint to go along wih her practical female wisdom. The old woman who brings milk to the tower in the 'Telemachus' episode of *Ulysses* is a believable Dublin working-class woman, but Stephen almost immediately mystifies and mythologizes her into a political, female embodiment of Ireland:

> Crouching by a patient cow at daybreak in the lush field, a witch on her toadstool, her wrinkled fingers quick at the squirting dugs. . . . Silk of the kine and poor old woman, names given her in old times. A wandering crone, lowly form of an immortal . . . .(1.400-4)

The 'Nausicaa' episode of *Ulysses* provides a good opportunity to consider the roles and discourses available to young middle-class women in the Dublin of Joyce's day. Gerty manages to be alone in her thoughts part of the time, but is also seen in the company of other young women and in romantic conjunction with Bloom. Like other single females in Joyce, she is damaged. Her limp corresponds to Maria's simple-mindedness in 'Clay' and to Issy's lisp and possible schizophrenia in *Finnegans Wake,* suggesting perhaps that female experience is as crippling as the male discourses we have examined earlier. The chapter is not an example of simple realism. But Gerty MacDowell shares the cultural situation of earlier, more realistic Dublin characters. Her home life and educational possibilities have been restricted by a drinking father, as is the case with Dilly Dedalus and the male child of 'Counterparts'. She risks the fate of spinsterhood which threatened Mrs Kearny of 'A Mother', and has overtaken Maria of 'Clay', and the Morkan women of 'The Dead'. Thus the discourse of attracting men is a major concern, as is her frustrated relationship with a boy on a bicycle, a failure she only gradually admits to herself. Gerty's juxtaposition with operations of child care and a church service suggest other female roles—mother nurture, the Virgin Mary (whose litany is featured) and the nun—and allows us to think about their relevant discourses. Gerty's thinking bears comparison with Molly Bloom's, in the 'Penelope' episode (*J & F* 179-81).

Gerty's discourse has been treated in the context of sentimental fiction, and specifically in comparison to Maria
Cummins' *The Lamplighter* by feminist Joycean, Suzette
Henke.[8] Henke notes echoes of Joyce's own sentimental
affairs in Gerty, and a parody of feminine socialization,
not an attack on Gerty. Gilbert and Gubar suggest, far
less sympathetically, that Gerty's resemblance to Maria
Cummins and 'the commercial crap of Gertie's [sic] genteel
Victorian diction symbolises a larger historical phenomenon
—namely the reaction-formation of intensified misogyny
with which male writers greeted the entrance of women into
the literary marketplace'.[9] Joyce came too late to be part of
this phenomenon, it seems to me. It is worthwhile, however,
to consider how Joyce makes use of the discourse of the
popular romance, in the light of recent feminist research on
women's reading and writing of that genre.

The 'namby-pamby jammy marmalady drawersy (alto
la!) style' (*L* I, 135) of 'Nausicaa' is not realistic female
speech. A narrator intervenes in Gerty's thought processes
and assumes the manner of magazines and novels written
for women living in a patriarchal society. Male-dominated
commercial ventures and many male authors co-produced
the heroine's romance, which commodifies women, and
directs them toward male-centring, and toward a romantic
quest. At issue is the basic romance plot which flourished
throughout the nineteenth century and still sells well today.
Joyce's satire of the sentimental romance novel and his
refusal of its ending in 'Nausicaa', *Exiles* and the *Dubliners*
stories we have noted has its counterpart in the efforts of
female modernists to write beyond the usual romance ending, a development in fiction explored by Rachel Blau
DuPlessis.[10] Reading or writing the romance has typically
been treated with condescension by academics, even feminists, as Janice Radway has noted in a study that incorporates
field-work among contemporary American readers of romances.[11] She deals sensitively with the ambivalences of
this fiction—its acceptance of patriarchal structures, yet its
demands for intelligence, 'spunk' and growth in the heroine
and nurture from the hero. 'Nausicaa' offers several elements

valued highly by contemporary readers of romances, including the development of a single male-female relationship (not the triangle featured in the male narrative of all
but one other episode of *Ulysses*) and, in Bloom, a nurturing male. Gerty, like today's readers of romances, finds
escape in the romance, and in her case the conditions to be
escaped are grim.

'Nausicaa' seems to offer an ideal community of young
women at its start: 'The three girl friends were seated on
the rocks, enjoying the evening scene and the air which was
fresh but not too chilly. Many a time and oft were they wont
to come there to that favourite nook to have a cosy chat
beside the sparkling waves and discuss matters feminine.'
The text goes on to describe the girls' charges, their
younger male siblings, whom they nurture and admonish in
turn (*U*13.9-13). This situation represents a repeated
female role in Joyce, as sisters and mothers mediate and
pacify the disputes of warring brothers or comparable male
rivals. Maria of 'Clay' seeks to restore harmony between
Alphy and Joe. Issy and ALP do the same with Shem and
Shaun in *Finnegans Wake*. In the opening skirmish of
'Nausicaa', the Caffrey boys do battle:

> But just then there was a slight altercation between Master
> Tommy and Master Jacky. Boys will be boys and our two twins
> were no exception to this golden rule. The apple of discord was
> a certain castle of sand which Master Jacky had built and
> Master Tommy would have it right go wrong that it was to be
> architecturally improved by a frontdoor like the Martello tower
> had. But if Master Tommy was headstrong Master Jacky was
> selfwilled too and, true to the maxim that every little Irishman's
> house is his castle, he fell upon his hated rival and to such
> purpose that the wouldbe assailant came to grief and (alas to
> relate!) the coveted castle too. (13.40-8)

The passage looks forward, not just to the conflicting
characters of the twins in *Finnegans Wake*, but also to its
frequent repetitions of the nursery rhyme, 'This is the
House that Jack Built'. Here it sets up the budding male as
master builder; his brother aspires to an even more phallic

and military structure, resembling the Martello tower. Cissy administers justice in the dispute as well as restoration: 'And in a sad plight he was after his misadventure. His little man-o'-war top and unmentionables were full of sand but Cissy was a past mistress in the art of smoothing over life's tiny troubles and very quickly not one speck of sand was to be seen on his smart little suit ... '(13.56-9). The narrative suggest that male militance ('man-o'-war top') is built into both language and dress for young Tommy.

At intervals, Cissy teaches Baby Boardman to talk. She first teaches him to ask for a drink of water, a lesson in demand; later, she places the father into his discourse by teaching him to say 'papa'. The narrator shares in stereotypical social values by stating the expectation that the bright, healthy baby boy will 'certainly turn out to be something great' (13.385-91). Even working in their own territory, and with ethics of nurture and peace, young women preserve the gender roles of males in society and discourse. It is part of this discourse that all of the young women bear diminutive endings on their names, as if they remain children.

Readers are left hanging for two pages before they encounter the last of the three 'girlfriends' on the beach. Edy teases little Tommy with the possibility that he loves Gerty. 'But who is Gerty?' asks the text (13.78). We soon learn that she is a different case altogether from Edy and Cissy, and that intimacy and harmony do not reign among young women. Gerty's thoughts throughout contain an implicit dialogue with other female voices; they assume envy, untruth and betrayal by other women, and a desire to be outstanding:

> it was not true that she used to wear kid gloves in bed or take a milk footbath either. Bertha Supple told that once to Edy Boardman, a deliberate lie, when she was black out at daggers drawn with Gerty (the girl chums had of course their little tiffs from time to time like the rest of mortals) and she told her not to let on whatever she did that it was her that told her or she'd never speak to her again. No. Honour where honour is due. There was an innate refinement, a languid queenly *hauteur* about Gerty which was unmistakably evidenced in her delicate hands and higharched instep. (13.91-8)

Gerty is embarrassed at the conduct and discourse of her friends, and she has little inclination toward mothering. Their 'squalling baby' gets 'on her nerves', as do 'the little brats of twins' (13.404-6). Gerty resents Edy's close observation of her display for Bloom: 'Edy Boardman was noticing it too because she was squinting at Gerty, half smiling, with her specs like an old maid, pretending to nurse the baby. Irritable little gnat she was and always would be and that was why no-one could get on with her poking her nose into what was no concern of hers' (13.521-5). Gerty actively plays the voyeur, a stereotypically masculine role.

Gerty's interests include art, or what she takes to be art—the poetry of Louis J. Walsh and the fiction of Miss Cummins. She is at least in part a parody of a younger Stephen Dedalus. She has aspirations to education, which have been frustrated. She looks up words like 'halcyon days' in 'Walker's pronouncing dictionary that belonged to grandpapa Giltrap' (13.342-3). She keeps a 'lovely confession album' in her 'scrupulously neat' toilette table, and has purchased violet ink (13.633-48), a colour well suited to Stephen's raptures over Gerty's precursor on the beach in *A Portrait*. She invents a romantic story to accompany Bloom's mourning suit, and a fictional future relationship for herself with Bloom. This parallels the formation of a relationship between Stephen and Bloom that many readers of *Ulysses* have sought:

> They would be just good friends like a big brother and sister without all that other in spite of the conventions of Society with a big ess. Perhaps it was an old flame he was in mourning for from the days beyond recall. . . . she would follow, her dream of love, the dictates of her heart that told her he was her all in all, the only man in all the world for her for love was the master guide. Nothing else mattered. Come what might she would be wild, untrammelled, free. (13.665-73)

Gerty's declaration of freedom from Society with its capital ess, and her quest for an ideal male form correspond rather well with Stephen's female quest and his societal mission, as we have traced them in *A Portrait*. Gerty's suppression of

sex suggests limited contact with men, a typical character-
istic of romance heroines,[12] and a meaningful social contrast
to Stephen's experience in nighttown. Gerty has a typical
allegiance to the church, and its service in the background
adds to the polyphony of the narrative. Conversion to
Catholicism would be a part of her programme for any
future spouse. The church service in progress reminds us of
the power of priests at the centre of Catholic practice. Gerty
has attended to these very priests and would delight at
being visited by them if she should become a Dominican
Nun. Gerty's text of freedom is undermined by her limping
exit, though the romance remains open-ended, even in
Bloom's writing of it. In *Exiles*, Joyce had attempted a
more serious writing beyond the romantic ending.

The play *Exiles* (published before *Ulysses* in 1918) sets
up a series of encounters between mature men and women
in a domestic setting where freedom from patriarchal Irish
marital norms has at least been attempted. A nine-year stay
on the Continent and Richard's denial of the institution
of marriage have made the Rowans' relationship daringly
unconventional by Dublin standards. *Exiles'* themes of
freedom and love are far removed from the discourse of the
pub, examined earlier in this chapter. Clearly the play is
dominated by a male figure, Richard Rowan, who has male
bonds, including the father–son liaison so typical in Joyce.
Richard's relationship with Robert clearly resembles Birkin's
love of Gerald Crich in D.H. Lawrence's *Women in Love*.
Richard has overcome many of the limitations of the immature male protagonist in *Stephen Hero* and *A Portrait*.
He achieves more conversation with his wife than Gabriel
Conroy manages in 'The Dead'. Mr Duffy, another social
non-conformist, had used his relationship with Mrs Sinico
to sound off his own ideas, brutally rejecting her on the
basis of her single, mild physical initiative in 'A Painful
Case'. Her punishment with death fulfils the patriarchal,
dysphoric (as opposed to euphoric) ending of a heroine's
text, as defined by Nancy Miller.[13].

Unlike the married women of *Dubliners*, or Mrs Dedalus
or Gerty MacDowell, Bertha Rowan has a variety of positive

interactions with characters of both genders. In his supple-
mentary notes to the play, Joyce imagines what Bertha
might have become, had she stayed behind as the wife of
Robert Hand, Richard's more conventional friend and a
successful Dublin journalist: 'Mrs Robert Hand (because
he intended to do it decently) ordering carpets in Grafton
Street, at Leopardstown races, provided with a seat on the
platform at the unveiling of a statue, putting out the lights
in the drawing room . . . , kneeling outside a confessional in
the jesuit church' (E 116). In short she would have shared
Annie Chandler's suspected materialism, E.C.'s suspected
respectability, and the allegiance to the church of all the
wives in *Dubliners* and *A Portrait*. She would have been
trapped in the marriage that ends the no longer satisfactory
plot of the romance.

Richard's greater maturity and his identity as a husband
have a biographical counterpart in Joyce, who had lived
with Nora Barnacle for eight years by 1912, the referential
date of the play. Joyce felt his shift from Dedalus to Rowan
was comparable to a new emphasis in Flaubert, itself a
response to economic factors in the audience:

> Since the publication of the lost pages of *Madame Bovary* the
> centre of sympathy appears to have been esthetically shifted
> from the lover or fancyman to the husband or cuckold. This
> displacement is also rendered more stable by the gradual
> growth of a collective practical realism due to changed econ-
> omic conditions in the mass of the people who are called to hear
> and feel a work of art relating to their lives. (115)

Joyce's responsiveness to the public's sense of their own
lives matches the gynocritic's response to women's interest
in realistic rendering of experience. I find it odd, however,
that Charles Bovary and not Mme Bovary should be considered a 'centre of sympathy'. Joyce's obsession with the
'cuckold' in *Ulysses* and *Exiles* still suggests a double
standard.[14] Nevertheless, the movement to 'husband or
cuckold' defines the male character by his relationship to a
woman—an identification that would never be taken up by
the characters we have surveyed early in this chapter.

Richard Rowan admits the benefits of his association with Bertha, telling his bachelor friend, Hand, 'Many ideas strike a man who has lived nine years with a woman' (42). Bertha takes pride in the sense that she has done more for Richard than the Irish, 'What have I done for him? I made him a man. What are they in his life? No more than the dirt under his boots' (100). Whatever Richard says about having formed Bertha, it is important to realize that, in her own opinion, she has also formed him.

Exiles has an obvious, frequently mentioned debt to Ibsen. It takes up his favoured themes of the artist in his relation to female subjects and the problems of marriage—both of which Joyce had discussed in a review of Ibsen's *When We Dead Awaken* (1900). As in Ibsen, argumentative dialogues present issues openly, and women characters express their dissent. Joyce sets up different combinations in the dialogues between his four major characters, allowing for variation of gender and personality. The fourth character, Beatrice, is the cousin of Robert Hand and considered marrying him as a young woman; yet she has a stronger mental tie to Richard. She resembles Ibsen's intellectual women. Richard and Beatrice have corresponded for eight years and he has made her the subject of his 'sketches'. Beatrice is comparable to the female figure of *Giacomo Joyce,* a student who became the subject of Joyce's own 'sketches', finished in mid-1914, but not published in Joyce's lifetime (*GJ* xvi). The *Exiles* sketches lie outside the work, but it would be interesting to compare Richard's imaging of woman to Stephen's bird girl or Gabriel Conroy's symbolic rendering of Gretta on the stairs in 'The Dead', both questionable renderings suited to male desire and mastery and their silencing of the female.

Richard has been the major force in shaping the terms of his partnership with Bertha, though both Bertha and Robert question those terms, and Bertha seems to have got beyond the control of Richard and even Joyce in some instances. Robert proposes to set rumours afloat to counteract public disapproval of Richard's unwed exile. He does this, as Richard charges, 'for the sake of social conventions'.

Robert adds, 'for the sake of.... our friendship ... also for
the sake of—your present partner in life' (39-40). Robert is
well aware of Richard's battle against conventions, including marriage. They had hoped that the house of revelry
they formerly shared (the setting for Robert's seduction of
Bertha in Act II), would become also 'the hearth of a new
life'. But Robert has worried from the start about Bertha's
place in Richard's life. He cautioned against her going
abroad with Richard and still questions Richard's fairness
and Bertha's freedom of choice. Richard responds, 'I played
for her against all that you say or can say; and I won' (40).
The response makes Bertha seem like the stakes at a male
game or a prize quested by the brave hero. Nora Barnacle
followed Joyce to the Continent on similar terms. Shortly
before their elopement, Joyce wrote Nora, 'The fact that
you can choose to stand beside me in this way in my
hazardous life fills me with great pride and joy' (L II 53).
But, speaking to Beatrice, Bertha (perhaps merely echoing
social opinion) claims less value: 'He is able to do something. Me, no. I am nothing.' Beatrice consoles, 'You stand
by his side', to which Bertha responds, 'Ah, nonsense, Miss
Justice! I am only a thing he got entangled with ... ' (100).

Robert would construct a more solid, traditional social
base for Bertha, and he worships her with flowers and talk
of the moon, a romantic sentimentalism Richard discards,
but that Joyce was capable of with women. Robert is in fact
wooing Bertha and justifies himself with the modern code of
'free love'. In its favour, free love allows no double standard.
Robert's 'Almighty' intended free love: 'You were made to
give yourselves to many, freely. I wrote that law with my
fingers on your heart' (64-5). The dialogue which follows
can be compared to discussions on purity that Stephen has
with his feminist friend McCann in *Stephen Hero*. Like
Stephen Dedalus, Richard finds problems with a single
standard for both genders. He balks at the idea that women
should give themselves to many and freely. Robert reinforces the notion: 'A woman, too, has the right to try with
many men until she finds love', and he speaks of ' a woman
who seemed to me to be doing that'. Richard would prefer

not to have heard of this sort of woman and sits with head
on hands when Robert reveals that he had known the
woman's husband intimately. This information confirms
Richard's expectation of betrayal by male friends, an expectation shared by Stephen in both *A Portrait* and *Ulysses*,
and a theme that links him to the discourse of the men
discussing history in the pub.

Richard attempts to define his own code for Bertha. He
states that 'I tried to give her a new life', but fears 'I have
killed her', meaning the 'virginity of her soul' (67). This
concept, and its effect on Bertha, is elaborated in Joyce's
notes:

> The soul like the body may have a virginity. For the woman to
> yield it or for the man to take it is the act of love. Love
> (understood as the desire of good for another) is in fact so
> unnatural a phenomenon that it can scarcely repeat itself, the
> soul being unable to become virgin again and not having energy
> enough to cast itself out again into the ocean of another's soul.
> It is the repressed consciousness of this inability and lack of
> spiritual energy which explains Bertha's mental paralysis. (113)

There are many problems with this theo-psycho-philo-
sophical explanation, some of them occasioned by the difficulty of adapting Aquinas' theories of soul and body to real,
modern situations. 'Soul' had traditionally been assigned
female gender in church writings. Bertha's soul has an
added feature, a female's investment in love. Joyce also uses
parenthetically the same general definition of love that
reappears in *Ulysses* 'The desire of good for another'.[15]
Bertha's 'act of love' as female outflow reverses the physical
flow of heterosexual lovemaking, but suggests an economy
Joyce continues to associate with the female, on through his
evocation of ALP as outflowing river in *Finnegans Wake*.
In Bertha's case, the female soul is an exhaustible, one-time
force—a limitation with useful implications for the male. It
suits his ego to have had this extraordinary gift, and it offers
some security from her betrayal with another man. The
paradigm also suggests a spiritual basis for the double
standard, the female simply lacking the energy of soul for

female free love, as envisioned by Robert. Joyce's later
sense of female libidinal economy would be less limited and
exclusive.

Richard suggests, furthermore, that the female needs
contact with the male both to think and feel. He challenges
Robert (who has wanted, more 'brutally' to 'possess' Bertha)
with a more constructive aim: 'Have you the luminous
certitude that yours is the brain in contact with which she
must think and understand and that yours is the body in
contact with which her body must feel?' (63). Implicitly,
Robert agrees that Richard has been an essential contact for
Bertha, that Richard has re-created her. Richard also claims
to have expressed Beatrice's soul for her in his writing (19).
Neither man admits to any need for female contact in order
to think and feel. Richard's power to infuse himself into
others, to re-create them, complicates the situation of love
relationships. Robert may use Bertha as a means of loving
Richard (the Richard in Bertha). Beatrice seems to have
loved the reflection of Richard in Robert, a quality that
faded after Richard's departure to the Continent. Richard's
plan for re-creating Bertha now seems to demand the giving
up of a second form of virginity, her fidelity. The notes say,
'to understand her chastity' Bertha must 'lose it in adultery'
(119). Richard's motivations are more selfish, as the notes
straightforwardly proclaim: 'Richard must not appear as a
champion of woman's rights. . . . He is in fact fighting for
his own hand, for his own emotional dignity and liberation
in which Bertha, no less and no more than Beatrice or any
other woman is coinvolved' (120).

Bertha seems well equipped to challenge Richard's plans
and paradigms involving her. Whatever the notes say about
paralysis (113), she emanates more energy than Richard,
especially by the end of the play. Exhaustion is more directly associated with intellect than gender, since Beatrice
shares Richard's fatigue in her chronic illness. Bertha works
with an explanation of love as a process of giving and taking
that is comparable to Richard's, but with significant differences. Perhaps her most interesting discovery (or charge) is
that love exists between Richard and Beatrice. We may

suspect Richard of a high degree of interest in Beatrice at
the start of the play, when he knows exactly how many days
she has been away (17). Bertha feels that Richard's letters
to Beatrice are his 'giving' of love. She also realizes that
Beatrice falls into a different category of woman from herself. Beatrice is more capable of 'understanding' Richard
than Bertha or Robert. Intellect, we might infer, is the
quality offered in conjunction and exchange by Beatrice.
But Bertha is also wary:

> You have given that woman very much, Dick. And she may be
> worthy of it. And she may understand it all, too. I know she is
> that kind. . . . But I believe you will get very little from her in
> return—or from any of her clan. . . . Because she is not generous
> and they are not generous. (55)

Bertha requires giving and generosity of both genders in a
love relationship, making her concept of love more egalitarian than Richard's. She may overstate Richard's generosity to Beatrice. For one thing, his letters started only after a
year of separation, a period of considerable suffering for
Beatrice. Bertha is alienated from Beatrice by class considerations, Beatrice's 'clan', the respectable middle class,
whose love was more sold than given. Beatrice's Protestant-
ism may also be connected with giving and taking, the
Protestants possessing the established church and control-
ling much of the commerce of Ireland. *Exiles* makes a more
definite point of their 'gloom, seriousness, righteousness'
(30). It is interesting that Richard refuses to 'take' Bertha's
ideas on these matters (53). Bertha's 'soul' is fine for taking,
but not her mind.

Although Richard's relationships are central in *Exiles*,
Bertha provides a sense of female relationships and female
community. Speaking of Beatrice to Richard she says, 'I
feel for her more than you can because I am a woman' (55).
In Act III, after first accusing Beatrice of sharing in public
disapproval of her, Bertha asks Beatrice for her friendship.
She reveals that she had long thought about her and always
wanted to speak to her in this way (101). She also discloses

to her the suffering she has endured for Richard, 'I gave up
everything for him, religion, family, my own peace' (100).
She finds beauty in Beatrice's long lashes and the sad expression of her eyes, turning her remark toward empathy
for Beatrice's own suffering (101). Bertha, in turn, receives
comfort from Brigid, the family servant. This older woman
reassures her of Richard's regard, 'Sure he thinks the sun
shines out of your face ma'am.' As a lower-class woman,
Brigid is more accessible to Bertha, and has been similarly
empathetic to Richard in the past. He had told Brigid, not
his own mother, of his love: 'I can see him sitting on the
kitchen table, swinging his legs and spinning out of him
yards of talk about you and him and Ireland' (90).

Richard's mother offers an interesting case in gender
definition. Brigid feels a certain triumph over her, disclos-
ing another female division partially attributable to class.
Mrs Rowan's hardness partakes of stereotypical maleness,
while Richard's father was soft-hearted and he remembers
him much more fondly. Both Beatrice and Bertha are concerned about Richard's poor relationship with his mother.
Bertha accuses him of never having loved her (52). Beatrice
does not like the way he describes her having 'died alone,
not having forgiven me, fortified by the rites of the holy
church'. That the church, and not he, should have given
her fortification troubles Richard. The notes to *Exiles*
suggest that Beatrice's mind has comparable church associations: It is 'an abandoned cold temple ... where now a
doddering priest offers alone and hopelessly prayers to the
Most High' (119). Here Joyce discloses his own distrust of
woman's relationship to a hopeless institution (Protestant-
ism being even more deprived of meaning for him than
Catholicism). Beatrice perhaps suspects Richard of project-
ing his sense of his mother's attitudes upon her.

One of the worst effects of the partnership Richard has
established with Bertha is its effect on her ability to relate to
others, including males. She fears that Beatrice hates her
(96-7). She worries that her detailed disclosures to Richard
may turn Robert from her. Robert does accuse her of ruin-
ing the men's friendship with her revelations (77). Richard's

leniency with their son Archie worries Bertha too. In comparison, she may seem hard-hearted, as Richard's mother had seemed to him (51-2). She summarizes these feelings to Richard, 'You try to turn everyone against me. All is to be for you. I am to appear false and cruel to everyone except you.' Richard realizes this statement takes 'courage' and says so 'violently' (52).

One phase of female experience and community gets into the notes, but not the body of *Exiles*. These notes prepare the way for Molly Bloom's reminiscences in *Ulysses*, and are based partially on the evidence of Joyce's mother's keepsakes, and largely upon Nora's girlhood in Galway. The notes offer a series of word associations to explore repressed memories of girlhood that are rich in female relationships. 'The blister reminds her of the burning of her hand as a girl. She sees her own amber hair and her mother's silver hair. This silver is the crown of age but also the stigma of care and grief which she and her lover have laid upon it' (119). Another series of associations 'holly and ivy, currant cake, lemonade' take her back to 'her grandmother's Christmas fare for her ', and her dark friend, Emily Lyons, who had gone away, and for whom her grandmother consoles her (121). In this 'homesickness and regret for dead girlish days' (121), 'a faint glimmer of lesbianism irradiates this mind' (122). The relationships of girlish days are all female, descending from grandmother to mother to friend, and women are left with a sense of loss. By offering Beatrice tea in Act I and a kiss in Act III, Bertha revives these associations.

Exiles is a confusing play because of its effort to sort out themes of freedom and the creation of character where men and women are co-involved. Its love quadrangle might be compared to H.D.'s novel, *Bid Me to Live*, which explores a similar structure of relationships, but from a female centre. Richard suffers in part from his own contorted theories. In the end, after resisting his theories, but involving herself in them as well, Bertha sets about re-creating Richard. He has wounded his soul for her, he says, and is tired. She has the last word, a coda form Joyce would use again with Molly in

Ulysses and ALP in *Finnegans Wake*. Bertha calls for selfless, mutual giving. 'Forget me, Dick. Forget me and love me again as you did the first time. I want my lover. To meet him, to go to him, to give myself to him. You, Dick. O, my strange wild lover, come back to me again!' (112). Bertha is not merely nostalgic. That was the trait of Mrs Kernan of the *Dubliners* story, 'Grace', who recalls the surface delights of her wedding; nostalgia was the trait of the male nationalists discussed early in this chapter as well. Bertha's recollections apply to a larger life principle. She would have Richard return to youth and wildness, as well as love.

Disappointingly, the other relationships recede for Bertha and Richard at the end of *Exiles*. Lost are the involvements with Beatrice, the intellectual woman, and Robert, the establishment man, who in a less exclusive arrangement might have transformed and facilitated transformation. There is a conservative reassertion of heterosexual monogamy, a theme also present at the end of *Ulysses*, which places both works into the tradition of the patriarchal, two-suitor narrative, where conventional morality demands the woman's choice. But desire has been redefined as selfless, and enunciated both in Richard's intellectual tones and Bertha's simple lyrical call. Richard has learned to doubt. The principle of 'incertitude' replacing authority moves Joyce toward new territory, narrative patterns and language that are more dependent upon the female and the unconscious, a direction we will pursue in his later writing, and with feminist strategies more attuned to the unconscious.

CHAPTER FOUR

Myths of Female Origins

Old father, old artificer, stand me now and ever in good stead.
(*P* 253)

The 'mythical method', which we are reminded of in these
final words of *A Portrait*, has stood James Joyce 'in good
stead', though it poses a number of problems for contemporary feminist theorists. T. S. Eliot coined the phrase in
the essay '*Ulysses*, order and myth' (1923), and in doing so
hoped to reassure critics like Richard Aldington, and even
himself, that Joyce was a classicist, part of a tradition, a
champion of order over chaos. Eliot heralded, not fragmen-
tation and experimentation, but 'a continuous parallel between contemporaneity and antiquity'. He was pleased to
have found a similar orderly articulation of myth in the
work of W. B. Yeats.[1]

To many feminist critics, the order sustained by these
male modernists is masculine. Sandra Gilbert and Susan
Gubar cite Walter Ong's suggestion that acquisition of the
classics is a 'male initiation ritual' and that since the four-
teenth century men have translated high classical themes
into the low vernacular shared with women.[2] As a young
woman Virginia Woolf envied her brother Thoby's classical
education, and took pains to learn Greek, a language Joyce
never mastered, though his Latin connected him with an
educated élite. The epigraph suggests that, in Stephen
Dedalus' case, order is invoked in classical Homeric style,

and organized by a father figure, identified with as a name-sake, Daedalus.

Eliot's classical invocation for Joyce is not unusual. Prior to Eliot's essay, in December 1921, the prominent French poet, Valery Larbaud, had introduced the Homeric parallels of *Ulysses* in a public lecture at Shakespeare and Company. The emphasis on classical tradition was sustained by Joyce's friend Stuart Gilbert, whose chapter-by-chapter study, *James Joyce's Ulysses* (1930, 1952), has supported generations of Joyce scholars with Homeric scaffolding. A bow—suggesting Odysseus' weapon—adorns the cover of the 1984 critical and synoptic edition of *Ulysses*. Although Eliot provided one of the most valuable endorsements then available to aspiring modernists, his reading of *Ulysses* and his representation of its working with myth are hardly definitive. Joyce has proven more subversive than preservative of patriarchal order to post-structuralist critics. He is as apt to parody as parallel the classics, as we have seen in chapter 3. Both Richard Ellmann and Fritz Senn have suggested that Joyce's Homer is hardly a strict parallel. Ellmann notes that Leopold Bloom pacifies Homer's hero, and Senn encourages a rereading of Homer in terms of Joycean remodelling of both classical texts and readers.[3]

While the classical, heroic Greek myths of Daedalus, Ulysses and Oedipus seem privileged in Joyce, his mythic archive is far richer. Ovid supplies, not just Daedalus, but also the story of Deucalion and Pyrrha, a male–female pair who shared the task of repopulating the world after a flood (*FW* 367). Significant female figures for Joyce include Athene, Persephone (*J & F* 199-200), Diana and Pandora. Joyce was much less interested in Helen than Yeats was, and preferred the domestic epic to the carnage of Troy. As noted in chapter 2, Joyce's first source for the *Odyssey* was Charles and Mary Lamb's version for children, a work in which Mary Lamb seems to have had a substantial role as author. Joyce appropriately scatters her name through *Finnegans Wake*, though as much to reinforce a theme of madness as one of authorship.[4] Another female mythological resource was Jane Harrison, a friend of Woolf's, whose *Mythology* is rich in female figures and was in Joyce's personal library.[5] The possibility that Homer was actually a woman writer was discussed by Samuel Butler in Joyce's day, and seems to have interested him.[6]

The Bible provides additional myths. The young Stephen is devoted to the Virgin Mary, but by *Ulysses*, she has become an unwitting vessel for Christ, experiencing ' a pregnancy without joy' (14.309). She becomes a servant to Stephen's theories of the word, as we shall see in the next chapter. The presence and importance of Eve should not be neglected. Anna Livia wends her way past 'Eve and Adam's' —a significant reversal at the start of *Finnegans Wake*, and a celebration of the generative female of the garden that can be found in the earliest version of *A Portrait*.[7] Mary Magdalene has comparable significance as the woman valued for her physical experience (an aspect which failed to discourage Jesus' love of her). Christ is less prominent in Joyce than God the father, whose role seems most appropriate to the aspiring author in Joyce. Stephen Dedalus or Leopold Bloom have been said to share Christ's suffering as dying god. It is not until *Finnegans Wake* that Shaun plays Christ obviously by pursuing the *via crucis* (*FW* III.2). Moses and Noah serve as father figures in family dramas.

Joyce's archive extends to Gnosticism which supplies the goddess Sophia, to Dante and his Beatrice, to Mohammed, Buddha and the Hindu goddess Shakti, and to the Egyptian figures of Thoth, Isis, and Osiris (*J & F* 198-9). One of his most elaborate systems of mythical doubles is Irish—the god Manaan, the goddess Dana, and semi-divine heroes and heroines of Irish mythological cycles, all reaching back to Celtic rather than Greek sources. Fables, legends and tales like 'The Mookse and the Gripes' and 'The Prankquean' of *Finnegans Wake* also border on the mythological archive, and Joyce mixes them in without giving the classics hierarchical prominence. Many of Joyce's traditional tales were provided by his father, including two *Wake* tales with paternal focus, 'Buckley Shot the Russian General' and 'The Norwegian Captain'. Joyce re-creates love triangles featuring a bypassed older male—Mark with Tristan and

Iseult, Finn with Diarmaid and Grania. Perhaps of greater interest to feminists is his mythologizing of local legends that border on lost history and popular culture—Grainne O'Malley (a woman pirate, as Prankquean), Biddy Moriarty (a famed Dublin scold, as letter-writer), Jack the Ripper, and psychoanalytical case histories, the most insistent being that of Christine Beauchamp, which is retold in Biddy's letter. Thus to charge Joyce with limitation to a narrow selection of western classical mythology is not accurate, though it persists, especially in comparative feminist work where the critic is unfamiliar with *Finnegans Wake*.[8]

Despite this diversity, the Greek connection weighs heavily for Joyce with many feminists. Gilbert and Gubar charge that *Ulysses* transformed 'a comment on Homer's epic into a charm that inaugurated a new patrilinguistic epoch'.[9] The model of Greek society is suspect, both for its domestic organization and its male ethos of heroism. William Herman charges that Joyce, like Eliot and Pound, was engaged in 'conserving the traditions of heroism, the manly virtues' in his handling of the classics, and offers Virginia Woolf as an alternative interpreter of the classics.[10] Philip Slater construes the Greek family as deeply misogynistic, displaying fear of the mature, sexual, maternal female, who is neglected by her male-oriented, absent husband, and resented as an authority figure by her son. He relates this psycho-cultural paradigm to the archetypes of Greek myth, including threatening females, like Circe, encountered by its itinerant heroes.[11]

Comparisons of Joyce to Woolf suggest that critics better schooled in women writers now hold up female standards in judging Joyce's creative achievements in the area of myth. Among his contemporaries, Djuna Barnes and especially H.D. were transforming myths; the practice continues with contemporary women writers like Hélène Cixous and Margaret Atwood, who are also notable for their feminism. We can use the mythical patterns detected in women's writing by critics Estella Lauter, Susan Friedman and Rachel Blau DuPlessis to pose a new and compelling challenge to the vision of Joyce. These mythical patterns go beyond those previously detected by such master theorists as psychoanalysts Sigmund Freud and Carl Jung, and anthropologists Claude Lévi-Strauss and James Frazer (author of *The Golden Bough*, an essential resource on myth for Eliot, Yeats, H.D. and D.H. Lawrence).[12]

Creative reworking with myth has been done by feminist revisionists of the collective unconscious concepts of Carl Jung, and by the French feminists concerned with psychoanalysis. Hélène Cixous has rewritten the Medusa and Oedipal myths from a female standpoint in order to deconstruct Freudian concepts of the subject and of family romance. Josette Féral reconstructs Antigone *via* the theories of Irigaray and Kristeva, suggesting that in burying her brother Polyneices, Antigone operates in the name of her mother, rather than observing the law of her father. *Antigone* is a favourite classical text for Woolf's female protagonists, from Helen Ambrose of *The Voyage Out* (which Joyce owned, but probably never read) to Sally Pargiter of *The Years*. As if to dramatize male possession of the classics, Sally has received her classicist brother's translation of the work. But she uses the classic in her own way, internalizing Antigone's experiences, and re-enacting her burial in falling asleep.[13] In *Helen in Egypt* (1961), H.D. moves Helen out of a temptress role. Her 'Eurydice', published by Harriet Weaver's Egoist press in 1919, resists playing the muse to Orpheus. Woman as 'temptress' and 'muse' are familiar archetypes in the criticism of male Joyceans, but insufficient to female modernist texts, and perhaps to Joyce's as well. Susan Friedman and Rachel Blau DuPlessis find alternative narrative forms in H.D.'s *Helen*. Friedman detects a psychological 'epic of female quest' that opposes a masculine world of 'strength, power, war, heroism' with a feminine image set of 'softness, flowers, gaiety, music, beauty'. DuPlessis sees an escape from the romantic plot.[14] Both alternative narratives can be found in Joyce. The censorship of H.D.'s work by Aldington, D. H. Lawrence and Pound is part of the little-known, insufficiently researched story of gender and modernism.[15]

Of special interest to students of Joyce's *Ulysses* is the

remythologizing of Circe in Margaret Atwood's Circe/Mud Poems'. Its second poem opens:

> Men with heads of eagles
> no longer interest me
> or pig-men, or those who can fly
> with the aid of wax and feathers

Thus Daedalus as well as Odysseus' men (transformed to pigs) are reconsidered:

> All these I could create, manufacture,
> or find easily: they swoop and thunder
> around this island, common as flies,
> sparks flashing, bumping into each other,
>
> on hot days you can watch them
> as they melt, come apart,
> fall into the ocean
> like sick gulls, dethronements, plane crashes.[16]

The hero's quest is diagnosed here as a disease, and Circe emerges from the mud as an insightful healer–psychiatrist, not a wicked sorceress.[17] DuPlessis detects sub-narratives of female writings and colonial power relationships, set against the heroic, romantic plot imposed by the male invader.[18]

Feminist critical interest in myth has been considerable, but so varied that it was difficult to situate on the feminist matrix included in chapter 1. The feminist mythic method has been most attractive to those working in the 'imaginary', paradigmatic ground of feminism, especially those concerned with concepts of the unconscious, hence its situation toward the bottom of the matrix. Marxist feminists tend to be firmly attached to history and revolutionary change, and determined not to romanticize pastoral paradises or non-human archetypes. Gynocritical emphasis upon cultural experience and literary tradition rather than upon psychoanalytic paradigms presents another important tension. Still, DuPlessis combines Marxist considerations of family economies and colonial narratives with myth; Anglo-American feminist critiques have used mythical characters within discussions of cultural images of women—Nina Auerbach's Victorian woman as demon, for example. The 'Madwoman' of Gilbert and Gubar is comparable. Julia Kristeva studies the elaboration of the Virgin Mother in Christian discourse. She finds modern disruption of this allows her to move into her own writing of the experience of motherhood.[19] The decay of the Virgin, literally portrayed in *A Portrait* may have functioned similarly for Stephen (*P* 162).

Part of the compensatory work of feminist critics has been to build the archive of myths, restoring neglected goddesses, and the Eleusian rituals that were so alien to Aristotelian rational order; they are adding the myths of non-Western cultures. Women writers are also creating new myths out of their experience, including their experience of maternity and the female body. Hélène Cixous rejects the requirement of an ending, the search for an origin, returns to the self and returns of investment in traditional myth.[20] Estella Lauter's efforts to detect female myths in formation suggest a female symbolic code. Instead of modernist nothingness or wasteland, there is 'a landscape teeming with interwoven form of life whose affinity with our own we need only to recognise to enjoy', a sisterhood with, rather than a domination of, nature. There are 'permeable boundaries' and an 'incandescent' female figure 'who exercises her agency toward a less repressive condition' and displays 'transitionality'. Feminist myth works without creating a dichotomy between knower and known, or an emphasis upon self.[21] DuPlessis detects dialogues between marginal and centred mythological characters, and a movement away from singular ego to a 'choral' protagonist, embracing diverse units of libido, like the multi-generational family and diverse friends of Woolf's *The Years*.[22]

In practical usage, myth can mean something widely believed in, but considered false by oneself. Feminists have dismissed as 'myth' much thinking that has limited female experience and imaging through such diverse institutions as religion, or medical science. Michel Foucault has sensitized us to 'epistemes' like the 'hysterization of woman' accomplished in nineteenth-century medical discourse ('ordering woman's body wholly in terms of the functions of reproduction and keeping it in constant agitation through the effects of that very function').[23] This is the language of the 'Oxen of the Sun' episode of *Ulysses*. The 'angel in the house' slain by Virginia Woolf in 'Professions for Women', and the accompanying preoccupation with female chastity also so evident in *A Portrait* fit this aspect of myth as well. The myth of masculine creativity—the pen as penis—is explored in female contexts by Gilbert and Gubar. This sort of myth has been dealt within earlier chapters more concerned wih cultural experience, and will not be emphasized here.

Psychoanalysis provides another perspective on myth that figures importantly in this chapter and in the later writings of Joyce. Analysts have theorized that the life of the child often parallels well-known myths. Freud accordingly selects the Greek myth of Oedipus to describe what he considered an essential passage in childhood sexual development (really only male development). He focuses upon incest and the blinding of Oedipus—a form of castration—making these essential elements in his childhood sexual narrative. Cixous, though working out of a Freudian tradition, has denied the emphasis on castration in Freudian/Lacanian interpretation of Oedipus.[24] But myths of the family, of 'family romance' persist in both feminist and non-feminist psychoanalysis. Relations to mother and father are viewed as central to the constitution of the individual subject by Freud, Lacan, Kristeva and Derrida. Freud also uses a broader paradigm of family romance to explain cultural evolution in *Totem and Taboo*, a work known to Joyce. Here the forbidding father, parricide, and compensatory worship of the father and his laws provide the mythic plot. Anthropologist Claude Lévi-Strauss also emphasizes patterns of incest, parricide and fratricide in his structuralist analysis of myth, adding the interesting category of the disloyal daughter, whom I also find in Joyce's Milly and Issy. The cultural historical paradigms of the philosopher Gianbattista Vico also display a family romance, including an ominous father figure. If Homer was the scaffolding for *Ulysses,* many interpreters feel that the cyclical theory of history of Vico proved an essential structure for the mythic dreamwork of *Finnegans Wake*.

The Homeric parallel in *Ulysses*, its many references to *Hamlet* and, to a lesser extent, the archetype of the dying god (rather than the restorative goddess) focused upon in *The Golden Bough*, have encouraged scholars to centre upon Stephen's search for a lost father. Much of Stephen's thought is undeniably concerned with the problem of consubstantiality with the father—a phenomenon he wishes to deny with Simon Dedalus, and which he probes in the sacraments and Shakespeare, as discussed in chapter 2. The loss of his mother in death is outside the Homeric and the Shakespearean parallels, yet crucial to Stephen's development as a subject.

Feminist psychoanalysts have worked within Freudian and Lacanian paradigms of the family romance to offer a theory of the subject with improved gender balance and orientation. Melanie Klein suggests that the rediscovery of the 'beautiful land' of the mother's body is essential to creative expression,[25] a sentiment echoed by Roland Barthes, and a line of development we will follow in Stephen Dedalus. Monique Wittig suggests another way that the female subject is constituted, focusing on love for an *amante*, a peer lesbian love, a phenomenon we observed in the *Exiles* notes in chapter 3. Freudian constructs of feminine masochism, passivity, castration and penis envy have been challenged since the 1930s, though recently Juliet Mitchell has reasserted the social (not the biologically deterministic) validity of the paradigms.[26] Kristeva reconsiders the Oedipus and castration complexes, introducing the special problems of the female subject's passage from oneness with the mother to the law of the father—the rejection of the mother constituting a partial rejection of herself. She works against the concept that the semiotics of the mother must be left behind in infant development, having provided a pre-language basis for entry into the symbolic. The constant injection of the semiotic into the symbolic order of the father is essential to its operation.[27] Woman's

exclusion from the symbolic order troubles other theorists,
like Cixous, Gilbert and Gubar, however, and it is a problem we will return to in chapter 5.[28]

An anthropological view of myth as an explanation of an
unknown but profoundly important or threatening aspect of
experience—the elements of nature, the menace of death,
the original creation of life, the unconscious mind—certainly
overlaps psychoanalytical myth. Awesome forces are clad
by 'primitive' thinkers in anthropomorphic (human), gendered forms. This chapter will consider Joyce's rendering
of the great mother or *gea tellus*, her Amazonian alternatives
and the problems and potentials of gendered concepts of
space and time. We will want to consider woman's space,
and her evasion of a spatial concept, as Joycean myths.

Joyce's mythical explorations of the construction of the
psychological subject greatly favour the male subject,
beginning with ones resembling himself—the male persona
of *Chamber Music*, the boys in *Dubliners*, and of course
Stephen Dedalus. Hélène Cixous suggests that the becoming of the subject is a perpetual theme in Joyce, starting
her analysis with 'The Sisters', but extending it to include Stephen.[29] This is a concept which helps us around
Stephen Dedalus' classic Aristotelian value of 'stasis', and
his apparent identification with the father, and one that
moves him toward the mythic principle of 'transitionality'
that Lauter has found in women poets. We have considered
the male cultural influences on Stephen's development in
chapter 3, and can leave his development in terms of identification with the father to Joyce's Freudian critics.[30] What
seems more controversial in feminist terms is his mode
of rejecting his mother and other women. Feminists, led
by Florence Howe, have been particularly troubled by
Stephen's viewing of female subjects like the bird-girl as
'other', as defined by Simone de Beauvoir in *The Second
Sex*.[31]

Stephen makes some rather artificial, literary constructions of woman as 'other' or distant muse that are less
constructive than deeper, psychological contacts that spring
from his mother. The artificial literary constructions show

the immature artist's handling of male-devised literary and liturgical conventions, and are what was found deficient in early feminist critiques. In *Stephen Hero*, when Stephen has his first significant contact with a lively, desirable young woman, Emma Clery, he finds her 'image' incongruous to his aesthetics and the verses he has composed: 'He knew that it was not for such an image that he constructed a theory of art and life and a garland of verses and yet if he could have been sure of her he would have held his art and verses lightly enough' (*SH* 158). Joyce had a comparable feeling of incongruity between Nora Barnacle and the image he had cultivated for *Chamber Music*.

Joyce's early verses idealize the parts of woman he has seen emphasized by the decadents (her golden hair [*CP* 13], her bosom, which is good for male reclining [14]), or in icons of the Virgin Mary (the sombre eyes, the snood, the colour blue [19]), or in Elizabethan songs (the 'merry green wood' and her 'pretty air' [16-18]). Joyce's maiden has a 'little garden' (21) but, unlike the stronger Eve, she doesn't cultivate it. She must be summoned or sung to as she sits at a window. 'Love' is a solitary male persona, who at one point in the cycle upbraids the beloved for destroying male friendship or perhaps access to a male god: 'He is a stranger to me now/Who was my friend' (25). Throughout, the adored but distrusted maiden is more absent than present, a distant object of conventional, not physical desire.

Stephen's musing on the unencountered, literary Mercedes is comparable. He finds passive brooding is preferable to interactions with real, noisy children:

He did not want to play. He wanted to meet in the real world the unsubstantial image which his soul so constantly beheld. He did not know where to seek it or how, but a premonition which led him on told him that this image would, without any overt act of his, encounter him. They would meet quietly as if they had known each other and had made their tryst, perhaps at one of the gates or in some more secret place. They would be alone, surrounded by darkness and silence: and in that moment of supreme tenderness he would be transfigured ... Weakness and timidity and inexperience would fall from him in that magic moment. (*P* 65)

The bird-girl Stephen views at the close of chapter 4 of *A Portrait* is gazed at (to use Irigaray's concept of basic Greek aesthetics) and rendered poetic, but she is not psychologically encountered. Compared to the *Chamber Music* girl, there is a slightly fuller catalogue of her body, slender legs and full thighs. But the dove she is transformed to was in *Chamber Music* and is a suspiciously religious icon; her likeness to the Virgin Mary is even more strikingly rendered. Though Stephen claims that 'her image had passed into his soul forever' and he experiences an ecstasy that is at least partly sexual ('His cheeks were aflame; his body was aglow; his limbs were trembling'), Stephen still represents a woman in conventional terms of the religious call to a vocation. His much-analysed 'Villanelle of the Temptress', with its reliance on eucharistic trappings, is a comparable failure. The eucharistic metaphor is troubling, not just because of its religious conventionality, but because of its mixture of spiritual selfishness with the implicit intention to consume the host.

A more significant journey into the unconscious comes after Stephen's bird-girl construction has vanished. He reclines on a nurturing mother earth, then falls into a sleep that is also a fall into a flushed womb through rose-like labia:

> He felt above him the vast indifferent dome and the calm processes of the heavenly bodies: and the earth beneath him, the earth that had borne him, had taken him to her breast.
> He closed his eyes in the languor of sleep. His eyelids trembled as if they felt the vast cyclic movement of the earth and her watchers, trembled as if they felt the strange light of some new world. His soul was swooning into some new world, fantastic, dim, uncertain as under sea, traversed by cloudy shapes and beings. A world, a glimmer, or a flower? Glimmering and trembling, trembling and unfolding, a breaking light, an opening flower, it spread in endless succession to itself, breaking in full crimson and unfolding and fading to palest rose, leaf by leaf and wave of light by wave of light, flooding all the heavens with its soft flushes every flush deeper than the other. (172)

The most defining event for Stephen as an artist is not the meeting of Bloom, but the death of his mother, which occurred some ten months before the action of *Ulysses*. Her final illness had been announced to Stephen (as his mother's had been to Joyce) with 'a blue French telegram, curiosity to show:—Nother dying come home father' (*U*3.198-9). 'Nother' had been considered an error in Joyce's manuscript and appeared as 'Mother' in editions of *Ulysses* until 1984. In terms of the lexicon and Simon Dedalus' intentions, 'Nother' is incorrect. But it is an extremely useful restoration to the text. Most basically it elucidates why the telegram was a 'curiosity'. Its psychological suggestiveness is even greater, however. The word 'mother' is lost in 'Nother', which contains 'no' as well. 'Nother' also suggests 'another', or 'another mother', universalizing Stephen's feeling of loss. The manipulation of the word repeats to some extent Freud's 'fort-da' experiments with his small grandson. As an event in language, it would seem to move back through symbolic language of the father to something 'other'—more primary, pre-language appropriate to the imaginary stage, associated with the mother, and located in the unconscious by Lacan and Kristeva. Like many deliberate errors with language in *Ulysses*, it suggests the fallibility (phallibility!) of the word of the father and of society's modes of communication. The male-centred psychoanalytic tradition would suggest that a young man's movement back toward his mother is a regression. I suggest, in agreement with Kristeva, that this access to the semiotic is a strengthening move (I am deliberately avoiding the use of progression). It puts the subject into touch with the unconscious, and allows him to perform a critique of the conscious world, and its word of the father. An alternative way of looking at supposed regressive behaviours of both Stephen and Bloom is to detect a strengthening of the subjective self through a process identified by Woolf as thinking back through their mothers, as 'nothers', which opens the way for our examination of mythical parallels.

Following his mother's death, Stephen is oppressed by a conception of the womb as death, a universal association

with earth as both planting and burial place and with the
goddess of fertility.[32] In 'Telemachus' it is the 'wellfed
voice' of Mulligan that hails the sea as a 'great sweet mother'
echoing the decadence of Swinburne (*U* 1. 106-7). Old
women, not virginal goldenhaired girls, appear to Stephen
in *Ulysses*, but they provide the means to his development
as a psychological subject. They persist in *Finnegans Wake,*
where Anna's best songs are sung in old age, and where she
is occasionally costumed like an urban 'bag lady'. The old
milkwoman is variously mythologized by Stephen, but as
'messenger from the secret morning' is usually identified as
Athene in disguise, Joyce substituting a maternal female
form for the male disguise (Mentor) offered in Homer. But
Stephen 'scorned to beg her favour' and is envious of her
interactions with Mulligan and Haines. His function is
merely to pay her. Athene seems to leave no message to
restore Stephen to father or mother. Yet, despite her 'old
shrunken paps' the milk she delivers is Stephen's best nu-
trition of the day (*U* 1.397-461).

Stephen's encounters with old women continue in
'Proteus'. Almost immediately, Stephen spots 'two Maries',
assuming that they belong to the 'sisterhood' of midwives.
He pessimistically assumes that their bag contains a 'mis-
birth with a trailing navelcord, hushed in ruddy wool', and
recalls that the woman who delivered him was a widow.
Their passage encourages him to think of the female generative function as an essential linking back of humanity. The
ultimate mythical figure in this scheme is the first mother,
Eve, whose fructive form is in great contrast to Stephen's
deathly view of woman.

> The cords of all link back, strandentwining cable of all flesh. . . .
> Hello! Kinch here. Put me on to Edenville. . . . Spouse and
> helpmate of Adam Kadmon: Heva, naked Eve. She had no
> navel. Gaze. Belly without blemish, bulging big, a buckler of
> taut vellum, no, whiteheaped corn, orient and immortal, stand-
> ing from everlasting to everlasting. Womb of sin. (3.35-44)

Stephen's 'gaze' and the patriarchal myth of Eve's sin still
distance him, however. Stephen's thought regresses from

matrilinearity to the patriarchal religious concept of the consubstantiality of father and son. But even here, woman is inserted. Elliott Gose has detected the 'magnificat', Mary's hymn of praise, in the portmanteau word, 'transmagnific-andjewbangtantiality' used to characterize Arius' thinking on consubstantiality (3.51). Another interesting insertion (or non-insertion) into 'Proteus' is Stephen's contemplated, but never-made visit to his Aunt Sara's house (3.61-159). The connection is discouraged from the start by the 'con-substantial father's voice'—Stephen's memory of his father's mockeries of the household. Significantly, the elder Dedalus' performance invokes the Icarus myth 'Couldn't he fly a bit higher than that, eh' and imagines that 'Jesus wept' over these relatives. This is another story of a missing mother, for in the unmade visit, Aunt Sara is missing, bathing her daughter Chrissie; Stephen's non-visit is restricted to the bedridden Uncle Richie. Perhaps because he fears that he cannot get back to his mother through his aunt, Stephen unconsciously rejects the visit.

Later in 'Proteus' Stephen sees a second couple, a woman and a man, cocklepickers. Stephen thinks more about the woman than the man, proceeding from specific details to an anthropological myth:

> With woman steps she followed: the ruffian and his strolling mort. Spoils slung at her back. Loose sand and shellgrit crusted her bare feet. About her windraw face hair trailed. Behind her lord, his helpmate, bing awast to Romeville. When night hides her body's flaws calling under her brown shawl from an arch-way where dogs have mired ... A shefiend's whiteness under her rancid rags. (3.372-9)

The first part of his construction makes her a scavenger, a potential resource. But she transforms into a sixteenth-century prostitute;[33] sexually she is 'rancid' and the 'she-fiend' that the Greek misogynists and the church fathers would have led Stephen to expect. She ultimately connects Stephen back to his deathly mother as the 'allwombing tomb' (3.402).

'Circe' provides Stephen's ultimate encounter with his

deathly mother,[34] but only after both he and Bloom have
experienced numerous interactions with the prostitutes of
Bella Cohen's brothel and a series of hallucinations recover-
ing their pasts and their unconscious minds. It is a chapter
rich in goddesses and transformations, including significant
transformations of gender, and allows us to examine Joyce's
remythologizing of Homer, in addition to family romance.
As might be expected, Stuart Gilbert carefully locates
Homeric parallels for 'Circe', quoting extensively from the
Butcher and Lang translation. He describes Circe as a
'legend of black magic', the magical herb, moly, given
Odysseus by Hermes in order to counter Circe's bewitching
'evil drugs'. Gilbert identifies Stephen's inebriation with
Circe's magical poisoning of the crew. He also compares
Odysseus' raising his sword to threaten Circe (as he was
coached by Hermes) to Bloom's raising Stephen's ashplant
to the shattered brothel lamp, while discussing the extent of
its damage.[35] Thus Gilbert's Circe is a worker of evil with
whom men must deal forcefully.

Joyce's adjustments of Homeric parallels may make
slightly different statements on power and gender that fall
closer to feminist myth. Stephen's possible poisoning, for
example, is by his male companions, not Circe's maids, an
adjustment that shifts violence from the female to the male
and is in line with Molly Bloom's thoughts about male
drinking camaraderie in the 'Penelope' episode (18.928-9,
.1270-1). Bloom's moly (identified as his potato) is provided
by his mother, not Hermes, and he cherishes this maternal
association, not the magic (it is in the possession of the
prostitute Zoe during his most severe crises). Bloom is not
necessarily in favour of colonial, heroic male quests. In the
stump speech he makes at Zoe's request, he denounces Sir
Walter Ralegh (*sic*) for bringing two poisons from the new
world—the potato and tobacco,'the one a killer of pestilence
by absorption, the other a poisoner of the ear, eye, heart,
memory, will, understanding, all'. He seems prepared to
identify the profit motive of more modern exploiters of
foreign lands, 'our bucaneering Vanderdeckens in their
phantom ship of finance' (15.1356-71).

Joyce's rendering of Circe and accompanying adjustments of gender also merit special attention. Circe in her most bellicose phase toward Odysseus as Bloom is masculinized from Bella to Bello, as many have remarked. While Homer's Odysseus is spared the humiliation of Circe's magic, the less heroic Bloom gives up his moly, and is made swinelike, and simultaneously a 'she'. The adjustment links animals and the female, and masculinizes the concept of power. This constitutes Bloom's second transformation to feminine form in the chapter—the first performed in diagnosis by a representative of a male medical establishment, Mulligan. Bella–Bello sustains the traditional threatening aspect of the goddess. But this is not the sole representation of Circe in Joyce's chapter. The prostitute Zoe diversifies Circe's character. Like Homer's Circe, Zoe sings and escorts Bloom into the brothel (Circe's hall, also comparable to the sanctuary of Astarte or Aphrodite). This stimulates a vision comparable to the Homeric goddess' landscape:

> *Gazelles are leaping, feeding on the mountains. Near are lakes. Round their shores file shadows black of cedargroves. Aroma rises, a strong hairgrowth of resin. It burns, the orient, a sky of sapphire, cleft by the bronze flight of eagles. Under it lies the womancity, nude, white, still, cool, in luxury. A fountain murmurs among damask roses. Mammoth roses murmur of scarlet winegrapes.* (15.1324-9)

Zoe's magic includes palm reading and the capturing of the moly. She is the first woman to perform a ritual dance with Stephen. She seduces Bloom to the extent of his offering an awkward, mechanical caressing of 'her right bub'. Homer's Odysseus clearly followed Circe to her bed, and lingered a year on her island. Joyce's Bloom is sufficiently egalitarian to think of male adultery as an issue.[36] Zoe is more benevolent than Bella, protecting the feminine Bloom from Bello by hiding him behind her skirts, and peacefully returning Bloom's potato. While she is hardly the 'fair-tressed goddess' described by Homer, Zoe comes closer to this aspect of Circe than Bella. The '*tawny crystal of her eyes, ringed with kohol'*,softens Bloom's smile, and she is given the lines from *Song of Solomon*, '*Schorach ani wenowach, benoith Hierushaloim*' that are a self-proclamation of black beauty to the daughters of Jerusalem (15.1318-9, .1332-4). But her beauty can shift to ugliness betokening death. Moments after meeting Bloom, '*She bites his ear gently with little goldstopped teeth, sending on him a cloying breath of stale garlic. The roses draw apart, disclose a sepulchre of the gold of kings and their mouldering bones*' (15.1339-41). Clearly Circe's cave, as represented in the brothel, is womb that threatens death. The spectre of Stephen's mother is well prepared for.

Daniel Ferrer has characterized the spectre as an archaic mother who acts as an 'intruder in the father and son relationship'. Standing alone, this interpretation would sustain the typical emphasis upon the search for a father figure in *Ulysses*. Here the mother seems a primitive association to be exorcized. But Ferrer works carefully with gender in the chapter, noting how forms of domination are masculinized in Bello as Circe and in the phallic looming of the mother's ghost. He sees the mother as a combined parent figure older than the Oedipus complex and supports this by noting the combined gender of the omnivorous sea, first used in juxtaposition with the mother in the 'Telemachus' episode.[37] Although he does not create a Circe as admirable as the remythologized healer of Atwood's poetry, Joyce uses her episode to purge his heroes, while simulaneously making important points about the effect of masculine power on the feminine. The transformational aspect of female myths and the sisterhood with nature suggested by Lauter are persistent throughout.

Interpretation of the family romance in *Finnegans Wake* has always favoured the struggles of the sons to take the place of the father, a dying god figure, though the sons uphold his law, as predicted in Freud, Vico and Frazer. The dying god can also be enacted by Shaun in the role of Christ. ALP's part in *Finnegans Wake* has been considered beautiful, but not central.[38] Dirges for the dead god, seen in Ireland as keening and shrieking, echo ancient female rituals performed at the temples of pre-Greek goddesses. While the mourning seems to focus on the lost god (Adonis, Tammuz, or Horus) the complete story includes the goddess, who has a temple and a garden or a grove of trees, often set between rivers. She has the magical power to retrieve and/or reassemble the god from the underworld where he has been taken, or the landscape, where he is strewn. Her rite of wandering, collecting and reassembling constitutes a quest too long decentred by narratologists and *Wake* scholars alike.[39] One such goddess was Ishtar, called Inanna by the Sumerians and worshipped as Queen of Heaven and Earth. Joyce could have encountered her, her eyes painted with kohl, like Zoe's, in *The Golden Bough*. Also in Frazer's account are the female ritual mourners of Tammuz. In chapter I.8 of the *Wake*, the washerwomen speak of 'Annan' (205.9). The pool of 'Innalavia, ... atween Dultas Piscium and Saggitariastrion' (600.5-6) suggests the Sumerian delta land and the goddess of heaven. Like Inanna, one of the washerwomen plants a tree in the bankside.[40]

Issy, in the rare times when we encounter her, is usually oriented toward father and brother figures, though she has a sister self and an entourage of twenty-eight girls. It is her mother who tells the only tales of the mother–daughter relationship. Late in the *Wake,* ALP reveals HCE's wish for a daughter, and her own satisfaction in having a female partner in discussion, having tired of the men's 'recitating war expoloits and perseorations':

> What wouldn't you give to have a girl! Your wis was mewill. and, lo, out of a sky! The way I tool But her, you wait. Eager to choose if left to her shade. If she had only more matcher's wit. Findlings make runaways, runaways a stray. She's as merry as the gricks still. 'Twould be sore should ledden sorrow. I'll wait. And I'll wait. And then if all goes. What will be is. Is is. But let them. Slops hospodch and the slusky slut too. He's for thee what she's for me. Dogging you round cove and haven teaching me the perts of speech. If you spun your yarns to him on the swishbarque waves I was spelling my yearns to her over cottage cake. (620.23-35)

If we can trust Anna's report, the daughter in *Finegans Wake* does not repress the mother, as Freudian analysis might predict. Yet Issy seems to find expression as a 'twin-to mine' mind, a split subject more than her brothers, suggesting that she experiences the division against herself predicted by Kristeva.

In discussing the psychoanalytical myths of the subject, we have experienced constantly the figure of the mother. There can be no disputing that Joyce evokes an archetypal mother in Molly and in ALP, and that with his emphasis on family romance, archaic mother–wives are indispensable. Joyce even makes Circe, as Bella, a mother. The Prankquean, one of the most independent, fabled female figures of the *Wake*, is an outlaw inhabitant of 'Woeman's Land' (22.8) who repeatedly confronts the male ruler, Duke Humphrey. Yet, as Margot Norris has noted, even she has maternal urges (she kidnaps his children on three occasions) and is eventually married to him.[41] Lesbian writing and criticism encourage us to search for alternative female archetypes that fall outside the patriarchal family. The category of Amazon offers one such possibility. The Amazon has until recently been decentred in archetypal schemes. In discussing the traditions of mother–wife versus Amazon, Diane Griffin Crowder notes that even feminists like Cixous, Kristeva and Helen Diner have privileged the mother–wife figure. Crowder turns our attention to the writings of feminist, utopian writer, Monique Wittig, for one Amazon alternative. Wittig enriches and redefines the archetype. She constructs a culture that offers an 'original harmony' of a 'tribal commune' immune from 'relations of inequality and power' and the slavery of a later and degenerate 'mothers' cult of maternity'. In her myths the early Amazons wandered in a garden; women who stayed in cities became the mothers of patriarchal society.[42]

Can the Amazon be found in Joyce? Working with the four-type classification system of Jungian analyst, Toni Wolff, Nor Hall finds examples in Joyce of the three types of female archetype that can be related by a system of difference to men (the mother; the Hetaira or companion to a man; and the medial woman, who usually serves as muse or medium for a male). Yet she can find no character to represent the Amazon.[43] Amazon visions seem to me very limited in Joyce. His communities of women are hardly utopian, though their problems are usually associated with situations in patriarchal territories and laws. There is something of the Amazon in Miss Ivors of 'The Dead', but her project of encouraging Gretta to revisit far Galway meets Gabriel's disapproval. The college girls Stephen meets in *Stephen Hero* and *A Portrait* lodge in convents or at home, both patriarchal institutions that instil the virtues of piety and virginity. Maria of 'Clay' works in a Protestant institution, surrounded by tracts and dependent on praise from her superiors. The brothel of 'Circe' is a female-run institution, but it serves a male clientele, including the priesthood, and indirectly supports the patriarchal family. Bella occupies a position above her prostitutes, and promotes her enterprise in hierarchical terms—'This isn't a brothel. A tenshilling house' (15.4281). She is willing to take financial advantage of the inebriated Stephen. She seems conventionally ambitious for her son, who is said to be off at a British male stronghold, Oxford.

I think that the female side of Joyce's myth of civilization, as traced through ALP's origins, does offer an Amazonian territory, if not an egalitarian society of female peers and lovers. The same territory was suggested in the notes on girlhood in *Exiles* referred to in chapter 3. In *Finnegans Wake,* we have some sense of what women do in a territory that is not controlled by or even entered by men, and of the mysterious appeal of this territory to men. We get fleeting glimpses of woman as outlaw (the Prankquean), or as watery wanderer in an ideal garden, before she descends to the city (ALP).[44] It is when she enters the city (or, more correctly, when it is imposed on her banks) that she becomes a victim, enclosed, and attendant to man. But she also emerges in death or sleep, through movement and merger as life itself. She takes and maintains man, but also leaves him—a fuller set of options than in the Amazon utopia. Unlike the heroic male Greek wanderer, she does not quest or keep any object. She delights in flow, as life itself.

Both Gretta Conroy and Molly Bloom prefigure this place and economy of flow. Gretta, in the wild west of Ireland had a romantic first love who died for her. Michael sang of a female outcast, 'The Lass of Aughrim', who perished with her illegitimate child, feeling denied by her lord, whose very affections resemble rape.[45] The song has a mythical message about the patriarchy, and its heroine might today take her place as outcast wanderer beside Kate Chopin's Desirée or Woolf's Shakespeare's sister. We cannot know where Gretta travels in sleep, as 'The Dead' focuses on Gabriel's self-conscious epiphany. But the female mythical parallels are taken up again in Molly Bloom, who flourishes sexually in wild places—beside the very obvious boundary of the Moorish wall in Gibraltar and on the Hill of Howth, a wild patch to the north of Dublin. As Norris has noted, Molly Bloom is far less mobile than ALP.[46] Molly fulfils the stay-at-home role of Penelope, and tends to be stuck in bed.[47] But I do see her as a wanderer. Molly's memory traces the geography of her domiciles. Memories of Gibraltar take her closer to real Ulyssean territory than Bloom has ever gone, despite his greater physical wandering in the course of 16 June 1904.[48] Her thoughts are moved along by the noise of an actual train's whistle. She recalls 'Lunita', her moon-mother, who wandered from family bounds to become a female version of the wandering Jew, and Molly becomes the moon, hurtling into space, at the close of 'Ithaca'.

ALP, Richard Ellmann suggests, emerged from Joyce's dreaming of Molly Bloom. In the dream, Molly stands, goddess-like 'on a hillock under a sky full of moonlit clouds'. She flings a small coffin after Bloom, saying, 'I've done with you.' When Joyce, 'indignant' strode up and 'delivered the one speech of my life', an explanation of the last episode of *Ulysses*, ending 'on an astronomical climax' she tosses the snuffbox memorialized in the Clongowes episode of *A Portrait* at him, saying 'I've done with you too, Mr Joyce'

(*JJ* 549). ALP has her own comments on the 'Penelope' episode of *Ulysses* in her 'Mamafesto' (Chapter I.5). She celebrates Molly's sexual dynamism despite the confines of a Homeric model of patience and the final control of male authorship:

> eighteenthly or twentyfourthly, but at least, thank Maurice, lastly when all is zed and done, the penelopean patience of its last paraphe, a colophon of no fewer than seven hundred and thirty two strokes tailed by a leaping lasso—who thus at all this marvelling but will press on hotly to see the vaulting feminine libido of those interbranching ogham sex upandinsweeps sternly controlled and easily repersuaded by the uniform matteroffactness of a meandering male fist? (*FW* 123.3-10)

The passage is not a simple one. It compares quantity of chapters in the *Odyssey* and *Ulysses*, and describes the designs of the *Book of Kells,* a manuscript of a patriarchal text, the Bible, copied and illuminated by celibate Irish monks. Most significant in feminist analysis, a female 'character' of a male author comments upon his earlier creation of female character. Joyce is aware of the problematics of male inscription of the female, and has ALP voice this. ALP seems to resist the patience of the final coda of 'Penelope', appreciating more a sense of sexual *jouissance* expressed in active motion and vaginal figuration 'the vaulting feminine libido of those interbranching ogham sex upandinsweeps'. Contrast to this the dullness and aimlessness of 'the uniform matteroffactness of a meandering male fist' whose pen has earlier performed a repetitive, decorative, quantified sex act 'of no fewer than seven hundred and thirty two strokes'. In response to his dream-myth of Molly, Joyce composed verses to be sung to the tune of 'Molly Brannigan'. Against Molly's sexual freedom is set Joyce's increasing blindness (which explains the huge writing of the manuscript).[49] Like the dying god, he appeals for the restorative powers of his goddess:

> May you live, may you love, like this gaily spinning earth of ours, And every morn a gallous son awake you to fresh wealth

of gold, But if I cling like a child to the clouds that are your petticoats,

    O Molly, handsome Molly, sure you won't let me die? (*JJ* 550)

ALP is aware of other mythical women of Joyce and, in one of her final songs, includes references to both Gerty MacDowell and the Prankquean (*FW* 607.32, 606.30).

Joyce calls upon the voices of two marginal women, the washerwomen at the ford, to retrieve the earliest account of ALP. As is appropriate to her wandering ways, her plurability and her rumoured past, their narrative is moved by questions, approximations, rather than facts. It is tempting to identify this as a feminine narrative form. The choral nature of their narrative is one of the characteristics found in female narratives by DuPlessis. Virginia Woolf's efforts to get back to lost female figures in *A Room of One's Own* are composed of a series of questions, juxtaposed with actions, her lifting and searching of successive books comparable to the washerwomen's vigorous smacking of laundry, their reading and washing of soil on cloth as inscription. Woolf's Mary Beaton also fishes ideas from a stream. Questions are posed throughout Joyce's works, but from male mouths, they tend toward catechismic or Socratic display. The washerwomen are not ideal figures from which to construct feminine narrative, however. They share voyeurism and the capacity to denigrate ALP with her sons. Through metamorphosis to tree and stone and thence to Shem and Shaun, they actually pass through nature into male embodiment. This breaking down of sexual difference is significant in its own right, and compares to the Bella–Bello transition.

The earliest news of ALP that one of the washerwomen calls for is who (and how) first penetrated her sexually: 'Waiwhou was the first thurever burst?' (*FW* 202. 12-13). The first responses range through history, and suggest she experienced multiple rape and that someone with authority gave her away—a paternal cultural right (and rite):

She sid herself she hardly knows whuon the annals her gravel-
ler was ... or how, when why, where and who offon he
jumpnad her and how itw was gave here away. She was just a
young thin pale soft shy slim slip of a thing then, sauntering,
but silvamoonlake and he was a heavy trudging lurching lie-
abroad of a Curraghman, making his hay for whose sun to shine
on, as tough as the oaktrees (peats be with them!) (202.23-30)

The wish of 'peat' to the 'tough' oaken lover is a quick
deadly curse founded on the long-term cycle of nature, and
expressive of empathy for ALP. But the probe goes back
farther to a pastoral Eden/Ireland:

It was ages behind that when nullas were nowhere, in county
Wickenlow, garden of Erin, before she ever dreamt she'd lave
Kilbride and go foraming under Horsepass bridge, with the
great soughwesern windstorming her traces and the midland's
grainwaster asarch for her track, to wend her ways byandby,
robecca or worse, to spin and to grind, to swab and to thrash
for all her golden lifey in the barleyfields and pennylotts of
Humphrey's fordofhurdlestown and lie with a landleaper wel-
lingtonorseher. Alesse, the lagos of girly days! (202.35-203.8)

ALP could not foresee leaving the garden for Dublin
(fordofhurdlestown), or the Norse or English 'landleaper'
who would grab her. The explorers and invaders plough
her labial waters in cruel invasion. The washerwomen
finally arrive at an alternative narrative, the tale that ALP
began 'where the hand of man hasneverset foot' (203.16).
The hand that stirs her waters is the priest Michael Aklow's,
a less violent and virile mating of the divine with nature, or
perhaps initially only the bliss experienced from his manual
stimulation of her genitalia. It seems in every way a mutu-
ally positive action for the 'bold priest' and Anna, who 'ruz
two feet hire in her aisne aestumation ... That was kis-
suahealing with bantur for balm!' (204.3-4).

While in Joyce's day the city of Paris was where women
like Gertrude Stein and Sylvia Beach flourished, in the
myth of ALP it is where she is a defensive, apologetic wife.
Michael Begnal discriminates between her wifely voice and

her river voice, which is characterized by 'rhythmic cadence, alliteration and onomatopoeia'.[50] ALP leaves the city at the end of *Finnegans Wake*, encouraging HCE to abandon social values: 'aloof is anoof. We can take or leave.' She recommends that they 'sit us down on a heathery benn, me on you, in quolm unconsciounce' (623.19-20, 24-5). ALP seems to be dying: 'The cry of Stena chills the vitals of slumbring off the motther has been pleased into the harms of old slalciters, meassurers soon and soon.' But this gloomy sense of chilling stones (walls?) and malevolent lawyers, is offset by the dozing mother's persistent, optimistic capacity for vision. While the wanderings of Bloom as Ulysses end in an exhausted narrative ('Eumaeus'), ALP still has life:

> but the voice of Alina gladdens the cocklyhearted dreamerish for that magic moning with its ching chang chap sugay kaow laow milkee muchee bringing beckerbrose, the brew with the foochoor in it. Sawyest? Nodt? Nyets, I dhink I sawn to remumb or sumbsuch. A kind of a thinglike all traylogged then pubably it resymbles a pelvic or some kvind then props an acutebacked quadrangle with aslant of ohahnthenth a wench-youmaycuddler, lying with her royalirish uppershoes among the theeckleaves. Signs are on of a mere by token that wills still to be becoming upon this there once a here was world. (608.18-28)

ALP feels her dilution into the sea with physical sensitivity as well as senile confusion: 'Or is it me is? I'm getting mixed. Brightening up and tightening down' (626.36-627.1). ALP's return to a fondly remembered sea father may seem a final betrayal of the female. Yet ALP has significant female connections all the way. She parts from HCE, leaving her daughter to take her place. She cavorts with Amazonian sea hags, the many seaside girls of Joyce grown old. Most significantly, she thinks of her origin with her mother, who takes the position of a sky goddess:

> For she'll be sweet for you as I was sweet when I came down out of me mother. My great blue bedroom, the air so quiet, scarce a cloud. In peace and silence. I could have stayed up

there for soaealways only. It's something fails us. First we feel.
Then we fall. And let her rain now if she likes. Gently or
strongly as she likes. Anyway let her rain for my time is come.
(627.7-13)

The passage returns the mythical mother from earth to sky,
where she reigned in Sumerian and other pre-Greek myths.
Rain unites three generations of the females in the natural
cycle of rainfall. The fall takes on a new and very old
pattern of grace.

The *Wake* records deities comparable to ALP's parents
earlier as 'the old man of the sea and the old woman in the
sky' (599.35), and with these offers 'Father Times and
Mother Spacies' (600.2-3). Julia Kristeva picks up on this
pair to introduce a feminist view of the future that reinserts
myth into history. 'Father's time, mother's species', as
Joyce put it; and, indeed, when evoking the name and
destiny of women, one thinks more of the *space*generating
and forming the human species than of *time,* becoming, or
history.'[51] Kristeva implies that Joyce does not situate
woman in history. In a feminist three-generation history of
modern European feminist theory, Kristeva assigns pre-
1968 feminists to a masculine, linear form of time. A second
generation rejected liberal individualism and linear temporality and took up an exploration of female psychology and a
related dynamic of signs muted by culture. Their theory
rejoins mythical memory (including 'mother spacies') with
a monumental temporality. Kristeva is wary of an 'archaic,
full, total, englobing mother with no frustration, no
separation, with no break-producing symbolism'. Though
second generation feminism unites with other marginal
movements, Kristeva does not believe that the archaic
mother offers a mythical unity or supreme power, and
distrusts such power. Kristeva hopes for a careful examination of the desire to motherhood that goes beyond Freud's
equation of a desire for the penis (power). Motherhood
teaches 'forgetting oneself' but this must be accomplished
'without masochism and without annihilating one's affective,
intellectual and professional personality'.[52] Kristeva's third

generation feminist looks for a 'demassification of the problematic of *difference,* and a personal and theoretical investigation of the potentialities of victim/executioner in each subject'.[53] In 'Circe' Joyce would seem to have begun this project with Bloom's and Stephen's hallucinatory experiences of victimization. With ALP, Joyce offers a mother goddess who charts her feeling as a dying subject. Joyce goes beyond difference by rendering gender in language as well as in social ways. He reverses gender roles and clothing, offers sexual mosaics, changes the gender of names and evokes a bisexual universe (598-600).[54]

Long before Kristeva, Joyce sustained an attack from Wyndham Lewis over theories of time and space. The dispute was long and complicated, but reveals that male modernists were not all of a piece. Lewis fancied himself more revolutionary than Joyce, whom he dismissed in *Time and Western Man* as a 'time' man. To Lewis, the 'stream of consciousness' and the Bergsonian sense of psychological time (*durée*) were particularly abhorrent. Lewis labelled the kind of time expressed in Joyce and also in Bloomsbury 'effeminate'. In *Satire and Fiction* (1930), he regrets Joyce's 'internal method', saying that it has 'robbed Joyce's work as a whole of linear properties—contour and definition in fact'.[55] Woolf, it will be remembered, celebrated Joyce's rendition of 'the dark places of psychology' in 'Modern Fiction'.[56] Lewis' *The Apes of God* contains a combined burlesque of *Ulysses'* 'Lestrygonians' episode and Woolf's *Mrs Dalloway*, in which a character very like Bloom follows the movements of a pub clock that functions very much like Woolf's Big Ben.[57] Lewis advocated space instead, and his space was clearly not to be connected with the 'mother spacies' we have found in Joyce. 'In contrast to the jelly-fish that floats in the center of the subterranean stream of the 'dark' Unconscious, I much prefer, for my part, the shield of the tortoise, or the rigid stylistic articulations of the grasshopper.'[58] Lewis favours abstract lines in space. On a larger scale, he is geometric, technical, mechanical, and profoundly urban. In his revolutionary journal, *Blast,* he decrees, 'Bless England, Industrial Island machine, pyra-

midal.'[59] He shifts the sense of creation to human production, disqualifying mimetic art and creation in nature;
as his early revolutionary visions fade, Lewis increasingly rendered the human mechanical. The gigantic
print of *Blast*, like the headlines of Joyce's 'Aeolus'
chapter, offer mechanical experimentation within a reading space. Lewis continues to have an appeal to geo-
metrical thinkers like Hugh Kenner, and to Marxists
concerned with human production like Frederic Jameson,
neither of whom has displayed much affinity to feminist
analysis.[60]

Joyce must certainly be considered a writer of the city
and a student of human production, but his city is divided
by the feminine river, which precedes, and eludes it, relent-
lessly depositing its own nature and challenging human
attempts at control and theoretical mastery. As if in response to Lewis' demands for 'the rigid . . . spatial articulations of the grasshopper', Joyce clad a time character
(Shem) in the carapace of the grasshopper for his 'Ondt and
the Gracehoper' fable. This hints that some combination of
times and spaces is possible. To Lewis' *Time and Western
Man*, Joyce responded with '*Spice and westend woman*'
(292.6) in the fable of 'The Mookse and the Gripes'. While
it still embraces the stereotypes of woman as sugar and
spice, or as West End London prostitute, this title invites feminist commentary on Lewis. Woman bounds the
end of the west, the patriarchal system gone to wasteland and fascism in the crises of the modern age. Her
'spice', or *jouissance*, may provide saving alternatives
to male modernist dullness, linear surface articulation,
and sterility. 'The Mookse and the Gripes' seems to end
indecisively, with the two advocates of space and time
rhythmically receding—'bullfolly andswered volleyball'.
They are watched by 'Nuvoletta' (New Letters, a female
future in writing, perhaps), but she has failed to dis-
tract them from their argumentative rites. She sighs,
'There are menner' (157-8). The scene continues, however, shifting to the omnipresent river, who reasserts
herself:

The siss of the shisp of the sigh of the softzing at the stir of the ver grose O arundo of a long one in midias reeds: and shades began to glidder along the banks, greepsing, greepsing, duusk unto duusk, and it was glooming as gloaming could be in the waste of all peacable worlds (158.6-10)

Into this setting comes another mythic figure, a powerful black female, composed by Joyce as a political entity in counterassertion to Lewis' classicism, sexism and racism.

Then there came down to the thither bank a woman of no appearance (I believe she was a Black with chills at her feet) and she gatheredup his hoariness the Mookkse motamourfully where he was spread and carried him away to her invisible dwelling (158.25-9)

The scene has affinities in modernist women's writing. It suggests Djuna Barnes' *Nightwood,* and Gertrude Stein's interest in the black woman in 'Melanctha' in *Three Lives.* 'Mother spacies' puts away male gloom and division like moody children, or so much dry laundry, and gets on with life.

CHAPTER FIVE

Gender, Language and Writing

In the name of Annah the Allmaziful, the Everliving, the Bringer of Plurabilities, haloed be her eve, her singtime sung, her rill be run, unhemmed as it is uneven! (FW 104.1–3)

The word was with Joyce in the beginning and especially at the end with *Finnegans Wake*, a text which has proved a paradise for linguists. It might be convincingly argued that the word was male. The *logos* of the Bible emanates from a male God, was announced to Mary by Gabriel (whose name goes to the protagonist of 'The Dead'), dispersed by male apostles (who become 'Mamalujo' in *Finnegans Wake*) and taught by Jesuits to Joyce and to little boys (not girls) like the one in 'The Sisters'. Almost all of the literary texts and specialized discourses Joyce alludes to or parodies in the 'Aeolus', 'Scylla and Charybdis' and 'Oxen of the Sun' episodes of *Ulysses* are written by men. Stephen Dedalus thinks constantly about words and names as a small child, works in a phallic model of 'dagger definitions' as an adolescent, and clearly has an ambition to master words. *Finnegans Wake* is standardly presented as the dream narrative of a father figure, HCE.[1]

Joyce's linguistic virtuosity in *Ulysses* and *Finnegans Wake* could be considered another example of male mastery and power of performance, an excess of author-ity. Sandra Gilbert and Susan Gubar offer Joyce as their primary example of '*avant-garde* fantastists of language' who

transform a common mother tongue into father speech,
thus soothing the modernist 'male linguistic wound' and, in
Ulysses, 'inaugurating a new patrilinguistic epoch'.[2] Joyce's
composition by accretion might be discredited as a material-
ist economy of acquisitiveness and retention, quite contrary
to the 'giving, dispersing' feminine economy suggested
by Hélène Cixous. Michael Begnal has called Shaun of
Finnegans Wake a 'voice of totalitarian authority'.[3] As if
acting out the part assigned to Joyce by Gilbert and Gubar,
Shaun (as Jaun) anticipates bad times ahead for men in
language:

> In the beginning was the gest he jousstly says, for the end is
> with woman, flesh-without-word, while the man to be is in a
> worse case after than before since she on the supine satisfies the
> verg to him! (468.5–8)[4]

Even if 'the end is with woman', what sort of a fate is it to be
'flesh-without-word' and sentenced 'on the supine' to satisfy
'the verg in him'? Jaun needn't be accepted as Joyce, or as
an authority. He does serve the purpose here of suggesting
that word play and syntax readily become sexual and
gender-marked in the *Wake*. Language also has to be read
several ways. At first glance, woman passively satisfies the
phallus; on second, she is the flesh outside (without) the
word, the verge, or border of male discourse.

Gilbert and Gubar are prepared to celebrate the fact that
'for H.D., a word is ... a sort of mystic egg that can "hatch"
multiple-meanings' that 'she punningly revises words to
turn "ruins", say, into "runes"', that 'all words, as she
meditates on them, become palimpsests'.[5] They are not
prepared to see Joyce's puns and word images (he even
hatches work/eggs, as we shall see) in the same joyous
spirit. Contemporary feminists' plays on words (as visible
in several titles of articles cited in this book) are usually
easier to read than Joyce's lengthy portmanteau words,
since we are typically supplied with parentheses or a slash,
to promote deciphering. Still, it is comparable deconstructive play. Though his words are more dense and elaborate,

Joyce's project with words bears many analogies to Virginia Woolf's. In *Mrs. Dalloway*, characters watch words dissolve in the sky, as skywriting. Her final artist woman, Miss la Trobe of *Between the Acts*, weaves a pageant of history, offering fragmented mirror images of themselves to an uncomprehending audience. Though she seems to fail with the central play she produces in the novel, she begins another. La Trobe sits alone at the end of the work, and on the margins of society. At first 'words escaped her'. 'Words of one syllable sank down into the mud. She drowsed; she nodded. The mud became fertile. Words rose above the intolerably laden dumb oxen plodding through the mud. Words without meaning—wonderful words.'[6]

Joyce offers much more than the male symbolic order, the word of the father, and the virtuoso author. Words verge and depend on erotic and generative principles positively associated with the river, the primordial mud and the mother; they are beyond male mastery. Women in late Joyce react to language and write their own, though it is hidden away, written over and tediously deciphered by the male authorities. *Finnegans Wake* analyses its own intentions with language, and here the emphasis is upon diversity and multiplicity of sign, language and focus:

> It is told in sounds in utter that, in signs so adds to, in universal, in polygluttural, in each auxiliary neutral idiom, sordomutics, florilingua, sheltafocal, flayflutter, a con's cubane, a pro's tutute, strassarab, ereperse and anythongue athall. Since nozzy Nanette tripped palmyways with Highho Harry there's a spurtfire turf a 'kind o'kindling when oft as the souff-souff blows her peaties up and a claypot wet for thee, my Sitys, and talkatalka tell Tibbs as eve: (117.12–19)

Language production takes place at the hearth, not in the academy, and it emerges from interactions of 'nozzy Nanette' and 'Highho Harry', from, gossip, 'talkatalka', tea and peat. Margaret Solomon has identified tea with propagation; it is female pee that wets the tea.[7] The tea as urine and the peat as a woman's panties suggest a telling of the female body, a return to Eve.

In chapters 2 and 3, we examined Joyce in a realistic range, noting Stephen Dedalus' reactions to *logos* as the phallocentric word in scholastic, academic and religious forms and in the oral discourses on history of the men of Dublin. Acquisition and imitation were accompanied by alienation, and a search for alternatives—some of them suggested by women. The Stephen who appears in *Ulysses* is prepared to mock his former writing, including a set of books titled with alphabet letters (3.139). In the later work of Joyce, we find experiments in semiotics, alphabets, words and narrative that suggest new forms and territories (or very old ones) identifiable as female. Except in parody, the norms of discourse are no longer observed in *Finnegans Wake*. There is still fairly regular syntax, which sometimes assists sexual play, as in Jaun's statement, above. Though realistically portrayed male characters and a free indirect discourse related to them dominate Joyce's early writing and the initial style of *Ulysses*, identification of point of view becomes increasingly difficult from the 'Aeolus' episode of *Ulysses* on through *Finnegans Wake*,[8] where character and gender identification are much more fluid and mosaic than in previous works.

Still, two manifold female entities, Anna Livia Plurabelle and Issy, have remarkable relations to language, which have been neglected until recent studies. Clive Hart plays down the 'sound' aspect of ALP. As a semiotic resource, the provider of an alternative language to the developing subject, the mother plays an important initial role in this chapter, as she did in the myths of family romance in chapter 4. We will be looking at ALP's relation to language in the 'Mamafesta' of chapter I.5, and her final songs of book IV. The washerwomen of I.8 can be related to 'womantalk', as described by Virginia Tiger and Gina Luria: 'chastising, advising, chattering talk by means of which women join together and sew and mend and patch and stitch the seams of daily life. Womantalk is this hodgepodge and colored afghan embracing the community which is women's own.'[9] Issy's language and that of her twenty-eight rainbow girls mixes socialized norms and forms with ancient rituals and attempts at corrective vision (*J & F*, 189–95).[10] The *Wake* records male scorn of the female production of language, the language bearing a perverse resemblance to the traditionalist Eliot: 'those gloompourers who grouse that letters have never been quite their old selves since that weird weekday in bleak Janiveer ... when ... Biddy Doran looked at literature' (112.24–7). Jaun, too, fears 'sewing circle' and 'salon ... of a blue moon day' (453.7–12). The female production of language in the *Wake* is filtered through the dream of the patriarch, HCE, but it retains powerful suggestions of another order of expression, distinct from both male language and dream language, as did the 'Penelope' episode of *Ulysses*.

In this chapter, I am going to be treating gender in relation to language primarily in theoretical terms, and in the unconscious range of the feminist matrix offered in chapter 1. This is not to dismiss the work that has been done by linguists like Robin Lakoff on language as actually used by women—concepts applicable to women characters in Joyce.[11] I shall be using gender in a non-deterministic sense, as in Lacanian psychoanalysis, Derridean deconstruction, or Kristeva's feminist semiotics. I shall also be drawing comparisons between Joyce and the qualities attributed to *l'écriture féminine* by Hélène Cixous and Luce Irigaray.[12] Virginia Woolf had mixed reactions to Joyce's *Ulysses*. Her admission that it caused 'spasms of wonder' and went back 'to a prehistoric world' I take as a recognition of the semiotic, and the words in mud of *Between the Acts*.[13]

In the broader category of female narrative, beyond what we have treated in the myths of chapter 4, I find less to do with Joyce, but also less feminist theory, the explorations being so recent and partial. Joyce inscribes the female largely in the flesh or in erotic narrative, a restriction Freud also makes in describing female dream fantasy, as Nancy K. Miller has noted. Men's dream fantasies encompass ambitious, as well as erotic wishes, according to Freud. One aim of Miller's theory is to locate ambition and alternatives to it in women writers' work.[14] As earlier chapters have suggested, Joyce was poorly read in women writers, both because he was educated in a deprived (all-male) tradition, and because he failed to take up the gifted female contemporaries who might have enriched his sense of women as writers of ambitious texts.

From the very first scene of *A Portrait*, Stephen takes note of his father's stories. But using a variety of his senses, he also carefully notices his mother's emissions. She has a nice smell; she plays music and encourages his dance, an art form usually associated with women in Joyce. At Clongowes Wood College, he remembers 'her feet on the fender and her jewelly slippers were so hot and they had such a lovely warm smell' (*P* 7, 10). She has an erotic relation to language. Her image serves his definition of the word kiss: 'His mother put her lips on his cheek; her lips were soft and they wetted his cheek; and they made a tiny little noise: kiss' (15). This begins Stephen's focus upon maternal lips.[15] Described as soft and wet, the lips suggest not just her mouth, but her vulva, and both are 'they' or two. Irigaray focuses upon the diffuseness of sexuality women experience in their bodies. The two lips of the vulva are only one aspect of the multiple sites and surges of female libidinal energy, as opposed to the singular identity and orgasm of the male's penis and corresponding phallocentric language.[16] The lips produce minimal sound, and no word. This is fitting as an aspect of female silence. Yet the sound which is not a word is onomatopoetic and becomes the partial source of the word for Stephen.

Mrs Dedalus elicits written words in the form of a letter from young Stephen at Clongowes; he is ill and wants to return to his primary source of nurture. Stephen asks, 'Please come and take me home' (23). This is classically Oedipal, but also offers an intriguing relationship between language and the maternal body. Stephen closes *A Portrait* with another female writing form, the diary, which contains a number of entries on his mother as well as Emma, but, at this stage, expresses a determined leave-taking.

Nancy Chodorow's revisions of the theory of the Oedipus complex suggest that young men are helped in resolving their desire for the mother by replacing her with the women they encounter as prospective and actual mates.[17] Stephen continues to read the semiotics of the maternal body in the girls and women he meets, and to note occurrences of silence and suggestions of alternative languages. His own imagery re-creates female pulsions and genital forms. Stephen notices water 'falling softly in a brimming bowl' at the culmination of chapter 1 of *A Portrait* (59). He reads, almost as language, the look in the eyes of a girl and the pressure of her hand; her non-verbal expressions have a fluid, soothing effect that reaches to his brain and body even in memory, setting a pattern for future reception of female semiotics.

> He could remember only that she had worn a shawl about her head like a cowl and that her dark eyes had invited and unnerved him.... Then in the dark and unseen by the other two he rested the tips of the fingers of one hand upon the palm of the other hand, scarcely touching it and yet pressing upon it lightly. But the pressure of her fingers had been lighter and steadier: and suddenly the memory of their touch traversed his brain and body like an invisible warm wave. (82–3)

Stephen's first encounter with a prostitute involves more communication by gesture and pressure than actual language on her part, or significantly, on his:

> He tried to bid his tongue speak that he might seem at ease, watching her as she undid her gown, noting the proud conscious movements of her perfumed head.
> As he stood silent in the middle of the room she came over to him and embraced him gaily and gravely. Her round arms held him firmly to her and he, seeing her face lifted to him in serious calm and feeling the warm calm rise and fall of her breast, all but burst into hysterical weeping. Tears of joy and relief shone in his delighted eyes and his lips parted though they would not speak.
> She passed her tinkling hand through his hair, calling him a little rascal.
> —Give me a kiss, she said.
> ....
> With a sudden movement she bowed his head and joined her lips to his and he read the meaning of her movements in her

frank uplifted eyes. It was too much for him. He closed his eyes, surrendering himself to her, body and mind, conscious of nothing in the world but the dark pressure of her softly parting lips. They pressed upon his brain as upon his lips as though they were the vehicle of a vague speech; and between them he felt an unknown and timid pressure, darker than the swoon of sin, softer than sound or odour. (100–1)[18]

Stephen begins with an effort to control the situation by speech but the prostitute's own 'vehicle of a vague speech' moves him to uncharacteristic silence, submission and almost to hysterical weeping. 'Hysterical', derived from 'hyster', the Greek word for womb, is a negative symptom attributed particularly to women by Freud; it has been rehabilitated in some feminist theory as an expressive and useful form for organizing language.[19] Stephen ceases his gaze and opens his brain and body to an alternative experience, which is articulated in terms of the female body's warmth, the rise and fall of her breast, the pressure of her soft parted lips, experiences darker and softer than the intellectual, moral or sensuous experiences he has known in the world, but reminiscent of his mother's early kiss.

Even during his reactionary period of self-imposed asceticism, Stephen is receptive of muted voices merged with female form, the *ubera* or breasts. He takes as his text the other-worldly 'Song of Songs':

A faded world of fervent love and virginal responses seemed to be evoked for his soul by the reading of its pages ... An inaudible voice seemed to caress the soul, telling her names and glories, bidding her arise as for espousal and come away, bidding her look forth, a spouse, from Amana and from the mountains of the leopards; and the soul seemed to answer with the same inaudible voice, surrendering herself: *Inter ubera mea commorabitur*. (152)

Stephen's soul is feminine in pronoun and behaviour. The final surrender unites feminine soul with maternal bosom, an expression of primal feminine affinity, even lesbianism. Stephen's production of language or art is frequently inspired by the maternal, female body, the muse as semiotician. In his discourse with Lynch, Stephen admits that scholasticism is not enough to go beyond asthetics to actual creation:

> So far as this side of esthetic [*sic*] philosophy extends Aquinas will carry me all along the line. When we come to the phenomena of artistic conception, artistic gestation and artistic reproduction I require a new terminology and a new personal experience. (209)

Lynch enjoys the sexual metaphors, but postpones the discussion—forever, as far as *A Portrait* goes. In the scene where Stephen composes his villanelle, the word emerges from the womb: 'O! In the virgin womb of the imagination the word was made flesh. Gabriel the seraph had come to the virgin's chamber' (217).

Stephen's openness to female semiotics as a marginal form of communication is in keeping with his feelings of marginality as an Irish speaker of English:

> —The language in which we are speaking is his before it is mine. . . . I cannot speak or write these words without unrest of spirit. His language, so familiar and so foreign, will always be for me an acquired speech. I have not made or accepted its words. My voice holds them at bay. My soul frets in the shadow of his language. (189)

Notably, it is the soul, the female aspect of himself, that frets. Stephen also recognizes that he has special and different things to do with words. He meditates upon a phrase he has made, 'A day of dappled seaborne clouds':

> The phrase and the day and the scene harmonised in a chord. Words. Was it their colours? He allowed them to glow and fade, hue after hue. . . . No, it was not their colours: it was the poise and balance of the period itself. Did he then love the rhythmic rise and fall of words better than their associations of legend and colour? Or was it that, being as weak of sight as he was shy of mind, he drew less pleasure from the reflection of the glowing sensible world through the prism of a language manycoloured and richly storied than from the contemplation

of an inner world of individual emotions mirrored perfectly in a
lucid supple periodic prose? (166–7)

Stephen's interests here, though not comprehensive of
Joyce, bear elements of what has been identified as male as
well as female literary form. His direction toward an 'inner
world' diverts him from the masculine realm. His multiple
interests, his fascination with rhythm, his willingness to
watch colours in the process of changing, and his 'supple
periodic prose' suggest multiplicity, fluidity and recycling,
aspects attached to the female body and female writing. But
the 'periodic' also suggests what Virginia Woolf called the
masculine sentence;[20] at this point Stephen aspires to the
exact and culminating phrase, a control of language and
desire for representation (though different in its inward
direction) that has been identified with male language.
Stephen's habit of imposing Latin on an encounter with a
young girl, *mulier cantat* (*P* 244), and mother love, *amor
matris* (*U* 2.165) is also questionable as a form of linguistic
distancing, learned through the church.

A full panoply of ambivalences over male and female
sources of the word is visible in Stephen's musings in the
'Monologue (male)' of the 'Proteus' chapter of *Ulysses*,
thoughts which are the prelude to his actual writing.

Across the sands of all the world, followed by the sun's flaming
sword, to the west, trekking to evening lands. She trudges,
schlepps, trains, drags, trascines her load. A tide westering,
moondrawn, in her wake. Tides, myriadislanded, within her,
blood not mine, *oinopa ponton*, a winedark sea. Behold the
handmaid of the moon. In sleep the wet sign calls her hour,
bids her rise. Bridebed, childbed, bed of death, ghostcandled.
Omnis caro ad te veniet. He comes, pale vampire, through
storm his eyes, his bat sails bloodying the sea, mouth to her
mouth's kiss.

. . . .

His lips lipped and mouthed fleshless lips of air: mouth to
her moomb.Oomb, al wombing tomb. His mouth moulded
issuing breath, unspeeched: ooeeehah: roar of cataractic
planets, globed, blazing, roaring wayawayawayawayaway.
(3.391–404)

Stephen has earlier identified the sands traversed by this inspiring woman as 'language tide and wind have silted' (*U* 3.288). She is many forms of woman. She is the 'handmaid of the moon', identifying her with the Virgin Mary, but in her labours and movements, described both in practical and ethnic language ('trudges, schlepps') and in cosmic terms ('a tide westering ... in her wake'), escapes the stereotypical churchly role of receptacle, servant and lady. The tides represent the female body; they are also internal, menstrual, periodic; she is flow. She is 'other' to the male, 'blood not mine'. Gilbert and Gubar resist Joyce's 'fluently fluid' women, ALP and Molly Bloom, and see their 'scatologos' as a product of misogyny, a 'Swiftian language that issues from the many obscene mouths of the female body'.[21] Their point would be stronger if 'scatologos', secretions, emissions, and excretions were negatively viewed, or practised and aspired to only by female characters in Joyce and not by Stephen, Bloom and HCE as well. Most interesting in relation to the creation of language is the play with language that escapes the word of the world, a rite that immediately precedes Stephen's scribbling words. He lips and mouths a kiss to his departed mother 'mouth to her moomb. Oomb, alwombing tomb.' The soft alliterative sounds and repetitive rhythms suggest semiotic pre-speech associated by Kristeva with the mother.[22] He is at first 'unspeeched', his noises resembling an interplanetary and primal roar; planets 'globed' as he was in the womb. It is cosmic imagery that Joyce will repeat in the descriptions of Molly at the end of 'Ithaca'. It reminds me of Virginia Woolf's old woman at the gaping mouth of the tube to the underground in *Mrs. Dalloway* (1925), and her comparable, ancient syllabifications. Only when he has finished writing does he think of his 'augur's rod of ash' and of 'manshape ineluctable, call it back' (3.410–13).

Another reference to the womb and the word is made by Stephen in 'Oxen of the Sun', an episode that takes the womb as its central symbol,[23] and works its way through a history of the language in literature. In keeping with this general attitude, Stephen glorifies the 'postcreation' of the word over its 'creation' in the womb: 'In woman's womb word is made flesh but in the spirit of the maker all flesh that passes becomes the word that shall not pass away. This is the postcreation.' Stephen also acts superior to Eve, accusing her of having 'sold us all for a penny pippin'. Still he admits filiation to her: 'our grandam, which we are linked up with by successive anastomosis of navel cords' (14.292–301). Stephen returns here to thinking back through his mothers (as Woolf puts it in *A Room of One's Own*), as he did in the 'Proteus' passage noted in chapter 4. 'Anastomosis' may seem an unnecessarily remote word to the reader. Yet it suggests fluid communication between individuals, the flow and recirculation we have been associating with the female. Perhaps even a new 'umbiliform' type of narrative. More conventionally, the running of one human into another suggests flow of semen from male to female.[24] But, in citing the case of Eve, Stephen calls attention to a generative flow from mother to male or female child. His notion of creation of the word depends on interpenetration of the sexes, a mutual easing of borders of the self.

In the opening of *The Madwoman in the Attic*, Sandra Gilbert and Susan Gubar focus upon the pen as the phallic empowerment of the male writer with the word. Joyce too plays with this metaphor. It is present in the stick carried by Stephen, which he playfully identifies as the augurer's rod in the passage quoted above. But as we have noted, it doesn't assist his writing. Perhaps expressing the sexual anxiety of the modernist male, Jaun has lost his pen: 'I'd write it all by mownself if I only had here of my jolly young watermen' (*FW* 447.10–11). The male writer seems to need sexual assistance (possibly homosexual as well as heterosexual) to make his broken pen operable:

> Open the door softly, somebody wants you, dear! Y'll hear him calling you, bump, like a blizz, in the muezzin of the turkest night. Come on now, pilarbox! I'll stiffen your scribeall, broken reed! (442.31–4)[25]

The 'semiological' is even coined by Joyce in the following:

She has plenty of woom in the smallclothes for the bothsforus, nephews push! Hatch yourself well! Enjombyourselves thurily! Would you wait biss she buds till you bite on her. Embrace her bashfully by almeans at my frank incensive and tell her in your semiological agglutinative yez, how Idos be asking after her. (465.8–13)

Here males share in sources of a mother language, instead of competing. The 'semiological' is taken on by the male to talk to the hatching female. Both the commodious 'small-clothes' and the 'yez' may remind readers of Molly Bloom.

Cixous urges woman to write woman, and particularly woman's body.[26] Her own writing places the emphasis upon erotic portions of the female anatomy. Luce Irigaray, adapting Lacan's terminology of 'imaginary' vs. 'symbolic' is more specific:

> But *woman has sex organs just about everywhere*. She experiences pleasure almost everywhere. Even without speaking of the hysterization of her entire body, one can say that the geography of her pleasure is much of her entire body, one can say that the geography of her pleasure is much more diversified, more multiple in its differences, more complex, more subtle, than is imagined—in an imaginary centered a bit too much on one and the same.[27]

Joyce's account of the 'Penelope' chapter of *Ulysses* to Frank Budgen discloses similar erotic emphasis, but also interesting attempts to equate words with anatomy: 'It turns like a huge earth ball slowly surely and evenly round and round spinning, its four cardinal points being the female breasts, arse, womb and cunt expressed by the words *because, bottom* (in all senses bottom button, bottom of the class, bottom of the sea, bottom of his heart), *woman, yes*' (*SL*, 285). But do Joyce's wordings of female anatomy satisfy a female imaginary? Particularly the crude slang of 'cunt' where vulva might be substituted. 'Yes' is questionable, the desired response to the phallus. Joyce seems to select the areas of female anatomy most exciting to him as seen in the long elaboration of 'bottom' by the author famed

for his 'cloacal obsession'.[28] Joyce rarely mentions the
hymen, the focus of Derrida's writing of woman. Margaret
Solomon identifies the number 2 with the labia of the vulva
throughout the *Wake*. Her male number is 3, an inheritance
from Freud suggestive of 3-part male genitalia. As we have
seen, contemporary French feminist theory concentrates
more on genital economies and assigns to the male a single
erotic site, the penis.[29]

The language of flowers is one way that the female body
is 'written' (as Cixous and practitioners of *écriture féminine*
put it) in Joyce, though it is not exclusively identified with
female writers. In chapter 4, we noted a passage in *A
Portrait* where a rosy glow seems to open into a meta-
phorical journey into labia for Stephen. Molly Bloom takes
up her husband's identification of her body with flowers,
'Yes he said I was a flower of the mountain yes so we are
flowers all a womans body yes that was one true thing he
said in his life' (*U* 18.1576–7). Bloom's gift of eight poppies
was effective in wooing Molly. As 'Henry Flower', Bloom
gives Martha Clifford a subject to write about, and he
thinks again of the affinity of women to flowers in terms of
silence: 'language of flowers. They like it because no-one
can hear' (5.261). ALP, in encouraging HCE near the end
of the *Wake*, describes her hands 'in the linguo of flows'
(621.22). Issy's accompanying girls are written as flowers
and flowers typically triumph over ruins in the *Wake*
landscape.

In *Finnegans Wake*, female identities write themselves in
several ways. This is somewhat surprising in the case of the
mother, whom we have seen written but not writing in early
Joyce. According to Susan Rubin Suleiman, female as well
as male writers offer a written, but not a writing mother.[30]
The 'Mamafesta' or hen's letter is probably the most obvious woman's writing, though there is constantly the issue of
forgery by Shem or Issy, or even T.S. Eliot, where the
language of 'The Wasteland' seems evident. The text is
written, written over and analysed, becoming a collective
expression of both genders, a palimpsest, an anastomotic
text. Shari Benstock makes the Derridean suggestion that

the hen's letter is a writing on the hymen, noting that the document has been buried in a womb-like midden heap.[31] The hen's 'scribblings scrawled on eggs' would seem to be writing on her children more than her own body. Or she would seem to be writing on her man. The text defends his sins. HCE is also the egg written on as Humpty Dumpty. The egg as word or creative process of the mother or 'vicociclometer' is explained in the following ambiguous, ambivalent passage:

> Autokinatonetically preprovided with a clappercoupling smeltingworks exprogressive process, (for the farmer, his son and their homely codes, known as eggburst, eggblend, egg-burial and hatch-as-hatch can) receives through a portal vein the dialytically separated elements of precedent decomposition for the verypetpurpose of subsequent recombination so that the heroticisms, catastrophes and eccentricities transmitted by the ancient legacy of the past, type by tope, letter from litter, word at ward, with sendence of sundance, since the days of Plooney and Columcellas when Giacinta, Pervenche and Margaret swayed over the all-too-goulish and illyrical and innumantic in our mutter nation, all anastomosically assimilated and preter-identified paraidiotically, in fact, the sameold gamebold adomic structure of our Finnius the old One, as highly charged with electrons as hophazards can effective it, may be there for you, Cockalooralooraloomenos.... (FW 614.27–615.9)

The process of 'hatch-as-hatch can' is one of recombination of elements—often male legacies of the past. Judith Johnston is troubled that the product is 'the sameold game-bold adomic structure' suggesting a return to male struc-tures.[32] But the analyst here seems male, and the effect of his overly scientific language is comic, comparable to the overdone scientific jargon of the 'Ithaca' episode of *Ulysses*. I suspect that the old structures are the ones most readily detected by the male analyst. The passage also incorporates the mystical methods of inscription and letter transport used by Madame Blavatsky, and the process of anastimosis, discussed earlier. Mother-recovery dates back to a 'mutter nation' where the flowers dance in ascendancy over the 'all-too-ghoulish and illyrican and innumantic' male civilization.

The sentence, derived from Edgar Quinet, is used in varied
form throughout the *Wake*.

One of the washerwomen we encountered in chapter 4
complains of 'porpor patches' in ALP's 'gown of changeable
jade' or her writing for HCE. Thus ALP also writes on
clothing, the texts the washerwomen read. 'Porpor patches!
And brahming to him down the feedchute, with her femty-
fyx kinds of fondling endings, the poother rambling off her
nose: *Vuggybarney, Wickeymandy! Hello, ducky, please
don't die*!' (200.2–7). The texts for defending and preserv-
ing HCE are hardly feminist. But Susan Gubar has encouraged modernist scholars to look at the language of clothes,
at blank bedsheets, and at cross-dressing modernist writers.
She calls our attention to 'Isadora Duncan posing as a
Greek Goddess in the Acropolis and Anais Nin dressed
up as a caged bird in pasties', as well as 'stately plump
Gertrude Stein' (an echo of the opening of *Ulysses*) and
'Radclyffe Hall tempting confusion with Dorian Gray'.[33]
Bedsheets, as texts of sexual coupling are noted by both the
washerwomen of *Finnegans Wake* (213.24–5) and Molly
Bloom in *Ulysses* (18.1124–39). In addition to having an
obsession with the female bottom, Joyce was extremely
interested in female clothes. He made distinctly misogynistic statements on the subject, to the effect that women's
clothes interested him more than the women themselves (*JJ*
631). Joyce's daughter Lucia considered designing clothes
as a possible occupation and Nora Joyce frequented Paris
couturiers. Gerty MacDowell is an extremely careful
dresser, and many of Molly Bloom's thoughts go to the
problems and possibilities of her clothing (*J & F* 170–1).
She has in fact helped the family over hard times by running some sort of outlet for theatrical costumes, as Ben
Dollard recalls in the 'Sirens' episode of *Ulysses*.

My favourite cross-dresser in Joyce is ALP, dressed to
kill, more or less, HCE's attackers.

> She wore a ploughboy's nailstudded clogs, a pair of plough-
> fields in themselves: a sugarloaf hat with a gaudyquiviry peak
> and a band of gorse for an arnoment and a hundred streamers

dancing off it and a guildered pin to pierce it: owlglassy bicycles boggled her eyes: and a fishnetzeveil for the sun not to
spoil the wrinklings of her hydeaspects: potatorings boucled
the loose laubes of her laudsnarers: her nude cuba stockings
were salmospotspeckled: she sported a galligo shimmy of haze-
vaipar tinto that never was fast till it ran in the washing: stout
stays, the rivals, lined her length: her bloodorange bockknickers, a two in one garment, showed natural nigger boggers,
fancyfastened, free to undo: her blackstripe tan joseph was
sequansewn and teddybearlined, with wavy rushgreen epaulettes and a leadown here and there of royal swansruff: a brace
of gaspers stuck in her hayrope garters: her civvy codroy coat
with alpheubett buttons was boundaried round with a twobar
tunnel belt: a four penny bit in each pocketside weighted her
safe from the blowaway windrush; she had a clothes-peg tight
astride on her joki's nose and she kept on grinding a somme-
thing quaint in her fiumy mouth and the rrreke of the fluve of
the tail of the gawan of her snuffdrab siouler's skirt trailed
ffiffty odd Irish miles behind her lungarhodes. (*FW* 208.6–26)

The designation of cross-dresser hardly does justice to this
fanciful variety and flux. This is another palimpsest. No
real person could wear so many garments simultaneously,
nor could she obtain many of the natural materials. ALP is,
after all, an earth and a river goddess, making an adornment
of gorse and a brace of fish fitting accoutrements. She is by
turns the sort of fashionplate that Gerty aspires to, and
the labouring male. Of male garments, we begin with her
'ploughboy's nailstudded clogs' and move on to military
epaulettes. Her knickers strike an American as masculine
garb, though the garment itself was becoming feminized in
Joyce's era in Europe. ALP's fishy apparel could be considered male-identified, as the fish or salmon is usually
HCE, while the river is ALP. The knickers are versatile
garments: 'bloodorange bockknickers' are reminiscent of
the red petticoats worn by the peasant women who frequently work the fields in the West of Ireland. The 'bloodorange' colour is both middle-eastern fruit and menstrual
blood. 'Nigger boggers' reminds us of the cutting of sod in
the Irish bog—almost always men's work, but also the
labour of slaves. Her ploughboy clogs will be useful here.

Joyce uses the word 'nigger' frequently in *Finnegans Wake*, reflecting the usage of his era, though posing problems of racist language to today's reader. Still, the merger of woman with black links gender, class and race. The fact that her knickers are a 'two in one garment' merges female genital pluralism with male singularity, while at the same time sounding like a sales pitch. While epaulettes might appear on women's fashions, they suggest a military uniform, suitable to ALP's present militant plans. A notable example of Irish cross-dressing is the uniform, complete with epaulettes, fashioned by Constance Markievitz, and worn by her in the trenches of St Stephen's Green during the 1916 Easter Rising. The pin used to anchor ALP's streamers is a motif in many of Joyce's descriptions of female dress, including that of Molly Ivors, the new woman of 'The Dead'. A tiny weapon, perhaps it is his Freudian gesture of equipping a woman with a little penis, or his representation of the clitoris. One of the merits of ALP's knickers is that they are 'fancyfastened, free to undo', an access to sexual activity, but one countered by 'stout stays, the rivals, lined her length'. Women's dress was altered to accommodate the bicycle in Joyce's youth, and this is suggested in the 'bicycles boggled her eyes', as well as the knickers. This and her 'hydeaspects' echo Molly Bloom's musings on female bicycle riding in 'Penelope', where she sneers at a priest's warnings about 'woman's higher functions and girls now riding the bicycle' (18.838–9). Bicycles and sex work together repeatedly as an irresistible pun to Joyce in the *Wake*.

The passage makes reference throughout to washing clothes, typical women's work, and appropriate at this point in *Finnegans Wake* since the passage is part of the dialogue of the washerwomen. The tunnel and 'luggarhodes' as well as the river write the female body. A final detail is the 'alpheubett buttons' which connects button, bottom, female sexuality and dress with the basic element of written language, the alphabet. Gertrude Stein's collection of poems, *Tender Buttons*, is an example of women writing seemingly the most insignificant part of dress, the button, but being 'tender', they are in some sense the buttons of the female body.

Alphabet letters are played with constantly in *Finnegans Wake*, where the central female and male figures have their representative letters, ALP and HCE, hidden throughout the text. Women are connected repeatedly with other alphabets than that of modern English, suggesting that they possess a more ancient, lost language. Reflecting back on the 'Penelope' episode of *Ulysses*, the *Wake* detects ogham writing, 'when all is zed and done' (*FW* 123.4–8). The letter that the hen writes or finds on the midden heap puzzles the male academics who examine it with the pierce marks it contains—perhaps another form of primitive writing not decipherable to the experts. The letter has also been stained with tea, or urine, suggesting a female writing from her body. Shem tries similar ink.

ALP uses the cuneiform alphabet in her own poetics, though one of the washerwomen disapproves, preferring common language to Hindu jargon, or telekinetics.

> Honddu jarkon! Tell us in franca langua. And call a spate a spate. Did they never sharee you ebro at skol, you antiabecedarian? It's just the same as if I was to go par examplum now in conservancy's cause out of telekinesis and proxenete you. For coxyt sake and is that what she is? Botlettle I thought she's act that loa. Didn't you spot her in her windaug, wubbling up on an osiery chair, with a meusic before her all cunniform letters, pretending to ribble a reedy derg on a fiddle she bogans without aband on? Sure she can't fiddan a dee, with bow or abandon! (198.18–27)

ALP's 'cunniform letters', are cunning in form as well as cuneiform. Cuneiform writing originated in the Sumerian culture that worshipped the goddess of earth and sky, Inanna, described in chapter 4. Their wedge shape duplicates the triangle or delta, the silted language of the rivers of Babylon and the world that flow through the chapter. The geometric delta represents ALP to her sons and is a fairly universal representation of female pubic structure. The washerwomen's own narrative opens chapter I.8 with print set in the shape of the delta as well. It is interesting that a purple triangular shape is what finally represents the maternal Mrs Ramsay to the woman artist, Lily Briscoe, in Virginia Woolf's *To the Lighthouse* (1927); Mrs Ramsay like ALP is associated with water and repetitive rhythms. As 'antiabecedarian' the listening washerwoman is a rebel against hegemonic male language. Again we have 'telekinesis', a process Madame Blavatsky said she used to transmit her theosophical letters, another alternative language cited frequently in the *Wake*.[34]

Women who work with more standard 'abecedarian' language in Joyce have varying results and attitudes. We have noted Gerty's problems and her problematic models, romantic novels, in chapter 3. *Finnegans Wake* shows great awareness to brother and sister pairs, and notes that Pascal, Renan and Lamb were all helped in their writing by their sisters (477.1–8). Jaun admits to having learned from Issy's letters of 'derringdo' (431.29–32). In the 'Lessons' chapter (II.2) Issy's writing is tellingly restricted to the margin— the bottom margin, the footnotes. But she proclaims her use of the 'girlic teangue' in the first of these (*J & F* 190–5). Joyce's women characters are writers and recipients of letters—a reflection perhaps of Joyce's correspondence with his mother, Nora Barnacle and Harriet Shaw Weaver. We have noted the important correspondence of Richard Rowan with Beatrice Justice prior to the action of *Exiles* in chapter 3. Milly and Molly Bloom are both letter writers, Molly sometimes writing to herself in boredom.

Martha Clifford provides an example of a woman who has some difficulty with her letter writing in *Ulysses*. Her celebrated letter to Bloom mistakenly uses 'world' where 'word' was intended: 'I called you naughty boy because I do not like that other world. Please tell me what is the real meaning of that word? . . . I often think of the beautiful name you have' (*U* 5.244–8). Martha's letter is apparently typewritten. Thus her errors may be more mechanical than grammatical or Freudian.[35] The world/word disliked by Martha refers to Bloom's erotic language in his letter to her, and betrays both a timidity toward sexual experience and an

alienation from the language of the body. Another suggestion the passage elicits is a female role of inscribing a
world rather than the word. Like Molly, who earlier in
the morning has asked Bloom to define metempsychosis,
Martha asks Bloom for definitions. She has an interest in
the aesthetics of words and dwells on 'Henry Flower',
Bloom's pseudonym in their correspondence. Martha en-
gages in limited naming as well, calling Bloom 'a naughty
boy', her words exciting him to new plans for the correspondence. Bloom's reactions to Martha's letter are quite
relevant to her use of words: 'Language of flowers. They
like it because no-one can hear. . . . Changed since the first
letter. Wonder did she wrote it herself . . . . Go further next
time. Naughty boy: punish: afraid of words, of course'
(5.261–73). Bloom attributes a silent language to women
('they'), and plans a use of words that will allow him to go
farther, wary of her assumed fear of words. Bloom is also a
grammarian. Martha has made an error in tense, 'So now
you know what I will do to you, you naughty boy, if you do
not wrote', which Bloom repeats in his 'Wonder did she
wrote it herself'. He has performed a similar correction in
the early scene with Molly, changing her 'It must have fell'
to 'must have slid', though only the narrator comes up with
the ultimate 'fallen' (4.326–9). Final interesting details
about Martha's letter are that it encloses another pin, perhaps her little weapon of forceful sexuality, and ends with
X's denoting kisses, but comparable to the hen's pecking
marks in *Finnegans Wake*, and reminiscent of Mrs Dedalus'
original kiss.

Bloom is more adept with traditional words than the
women of *Ulysses*, but it is interesting that Joyce chose
as his hero a man who often has to search through his
mind for a while before coming up with the 'correct' word,
and his rummaging through words creates much of the
delight of *Ulysses*. As with Martha the 'wrong' word
(world) may be more significant. Molly undermines much
of the authority Bloom would seem to have with traditional words, just as the washerwoman calls for *'franca
langua'*:

—Metempsychosis, he said, frowning. It's Greek: from the
Greek. That means the transmigration of souls. —O, rocks!
she said. Tell us in plain words. (4.341-3)

The narrator of 'Cyclops' faults him for the same tendency,
as we have seen in chapter 2. Molly has a very lively sense
of words. She doesn't just ask for the meaning of metempsychosis, she personifies the word, perhaps significantly,
as a 'he':

—Metempsychosis? —Yes. Who's he when he's at home?
(4.339-40)

Molly has boggled the minds of generations of scholars with
her indefinite use of the male pronoun, generalizing male
actions rather than specifically representing them. Bloom
appreciates the multiplicity of meaning accomplished by
such descriptions as Bob Doran, the 'base barreltone'
(11.1011). Molly's 'errors' can be as productive as Martha
Clifford's, as for example in her confusion of omission for
emission in the language of a male gynaecologist: 'asking
me had I frequent omissions where do those old fellows get
all the words they have omissions with his shortsighted eyes
on me cocked sideways . . . ' (18.1169-71). Reading Molly's
body, we see the importance of the omissions of the emissions of her monologue, which is accompanied by menstrual flow. She, Martha and Bloom are all subject to
Joyce's arrangement of language, but in this arrangement
correctness of language loses its authority.

Woman's language has some variants in Joyce. It may be
as ancient as the cuneiform wedge or as common as Molly's
lingua franca. It makes do with available surfaces, an egg or
a rock. It is an essential variant for the male writer, and
allows him a measure of self-criticism. Female modernism,
as constructed by Joyce, does not show off with densities
and portmanteau words: 'But how many of her readers
realise that she is not out to dizzledazzle with a graith
uncouthrement of postmantuam glasseries from the lapins
and the grigs' (*FW* 112.36-113.2). Though he may raise a

'meandering male fist' of control, the action is sure to be mocked by his own female writer. Female language may flow in and from the body, or be woven or played as music. The aesthetic of women's language is sufficiently broad to embrace both the goddess and Stephen Dedalus in the artistic life-sustaining process: 'As we, or mother Dana, weave and unweave our bodies, Stephen said, from day to day, their molecules shuttled to and fro, so does the artist weave and unweave his image' (U 9.376–8). We find ALP a musician-weaver. 'Windaug', she weaves like Penelope, making music as did Mrs Dedalus in Stephen's first perceptions of her. She also unweaves, flowing away into impersonality and recombination of gender, as she rejoins her sky mother and sea father. ALP is allowed lush sound, but no personal ambition. There is no culminating, final sentence. Her language is as interrupted, interruptable as the final half-sentence of *Finnegans Wake*.[36] Yet her feminine language is what provides the umbilicus, the 'vicus' of recirculation and offers a new politics of relationship and authorship. As she flows to the sea, Anna thinks of the writer of 'work in progress' (the working title Joyce used for *Finnegans Wake*) and says with confidence, 'But it's by this route he'll come some morrow' (625.13–14).

Anna's route cannot fully satisfy the woman writer or gynocritic who has a shaping vision, a self-defining ambition and tradition, along with her physical female form, to equate with language. Still, the French feminist paradigms of writing the feminine enrich our reading of Joyce, taking us beyond Freud and beyond structuralism. A troubling possibility is that Joyce's writing of woman still serves a male author's ego, proving he can move into 'other' forms. On the other hand, if the move is made, not in the spirit of epic conquest, but as wanderer-gatherer and re-viewer of writing, we should wish for more male writers who will follow in Anna's wake.

Notes

Preface and Acknowledgements

1. Virginia Woolf, *Jacob's Room*, 106–7. Julia thinks, as she examines the names circling the dome of the British Museum, 'Oh damn . . . why didn't they leave room for an Eliot or a Brontë?' She also finds Jacob Flanders' library labours far simpler than hers: 'When her books came she applied herself to her gigantic labours, but perceived through one of the nerves of her exasperated sensibility how composedly, unconcernedly, and with every consideration the male readers applied themselves to theirs. That young man for example. What had he to do except copy out poetry? And she must study statistics.'

Chapter One Plurabilities

1. In my opinion, Margot Norris' *The Decentered Universe of Finnegans Wake* was the first theoretical book by a woman scholar received enthusiastically. Several women scholars had been modestly praised for competent scholarship and criticism. The James Joyce Foundation and the *James Joyce Quarterly* have always been headed by men. A Women's Caucus of the Foundation was organized in 1982. In 1985, membership of women scholars on the foundation's board of trustees increased to 4 (previously there was 1). Recent symposia have offered increasing numbers of feminist papers and sessions.
2. Virginia Woolf goes so far as to ritually burn the word 'feminist'. *Three Guineas*, 101–2.
3. An excellent assessment of the value male theorists have attached to feminist deconstructive work is Bernard Duyfhuizen's review essay 'Deconstruction and feminist literary theory', *Tulsa Studies in*

130

Women's Literature, 3.1/2 (1984), 159/67. In the same issue, Jane Marcus assesses male critics' attempts to read as feminists, and their failure to give credit for feminist theory. See 'Still practice, a/wrested alphabet: toward a feminist aesthetic'. Jonathan Culler gives serious attention to female theoreticians and offers a chapter on 'Reading as a Woman' in his *On Deconstruction*.

4. Gayatri Spivak speaks of her participation in three marginal critical movements: feminism, Marxism and deconstruction in 'Feminism and critical theory', *Women's Studies International Quarterly*, 1.3 (1978), 241–6.

5. See my 'Introduction: Joyce Studies 1985', in *New Alliances in Joyce Studies*, ed Bonnie Kime Scott.

6. Showalter, 'Feminist criticism in the wilderness', *Critical Inquiry*, 8.2 (Winter 1981), 184–7. Showalter pioneered this practice in her influential *A Literature of their Own*.

7. Showalter, 'Wilderness', 185. I do not include French practices as gynocriticism, though Showalter suggests this.

8. At present there is one collection of female-centred essays, *Women in Joyce* (1982). Many of these focus on individual female characters or develop a sense of women's culture in Dublin. Suzette Henke applies the theories of Kristeva and Foucault, as well as archetypal criticism in her excellent study, 'Stephen Dedalus and women: a portrait of the artist as a young misogynist' (82–107). My *Joyce and Feminism* (1984) was the first study by a single author. Feminist insights of a structuralist nature are available in Margot Norris' *The Decentered Universe of Finnegans Wake* (1974). Colin MacCabe works with gender throughout his post-structuralist *James Joyce and the Revolution of the Word* (1979). Marilyn French's *The Book as World* (1975) displays liberal, humanistic feminism throughout, and evaluates the gendered narrative structure achieved by Molly Bloom's final monologue. See *J & F* 108–32. Forthcoming volumes based on Joyce symposia should be consulted for feminist contents. Additional Joycean feminist articles are cited in the course of this book.

9. *Sexual/Textual Politics*, 50–6, 75–9.

10. See *Toward a Balanced Curriculum*, ed Bonnie Spanier, Alexander Bloom and Darlene Boroviak.

11. They are termed 'gynesis' as a distinction from gynocriticism by Alice Jardine, 'Gynesis,' *Diacritics*, 7/8 (1978), 54–65.

12. 'The future of feminist criticism', in *Feminist Literary Criticism*, 71–3, 76. Showalter's current emphasis on women critics is expressed in her selection and her introduction to *The New Feminist Criticism*, 4–5.

13. *A Literature of their Own*, 282–97.

14. 'Sexual linguistics: gender, language, sexuality', *New Literary History*, 16.3 (1985), 521, 535.

15. Annette Kolodny, 'A map for rereading: or, gender and the interpretation of literary texts', *New Literary History*, 2 (Spring 1980), 451–467.

16. See *Woman and Nature* and 'The way of all ideology', *Signs*, 7.3 (1982), 641–60.
17. See 'This sex which is not one', in *New French Feminisms: An Anthology*, ed Elaine Marks and Isabelle de Courtivron, 101.
18. Marks, 'Woman and literature', 840.
19. Christiane Makward, 'Interview with Hélène Cixous', trans. Ann Liddle and Beatrice Cameron, *Sub Stance*, 13 (1976), 31.
20. 'Castration or decapitation?', 53.
21. 'Wilderness', 69.
22. Marxist-Feminist Literature Collective, 'Women's writing: Jane Eyre, Shirley, Villette, Aurora Leigh', *Ideology and Consciousness*, 3 (Spring 1978), 28.
23. For a good summary, see Juliet Mitchell and Jacqueline Rose (eds), *Feminine Sexuality: Jacques Lacan and the Ecole Freudienne*, 14.
24. Hélène Cixous, 'Castration or decapitation?' *Signs*, 7.1 (1981), 41–55. For my summary of Lacan, I am indebted to Toril Moi. See *Sexual/Textual Politics*, 161–3.
25. Luce Irigaray, has written critiques of both Freud and Lacan. Her objections to the latter, like those of Cixous, centre upon the negative value he gives to women in relation to language. See *Speculum de l'autre femme* and 'This sex which is not one'. Also on Freud, see Jane Gallop, *Feminism and Psychoanalysis: The Daughter's Seduction*, 56–79.
26. 'Women's time', 33–5.
27. Leon S. Roudiez, 'Introduction', *Desire in Language* by Julia Kristeva, 6.
28. 'Woman's time', 15–16.
29. Annette Kolodny, 'Dancing through the minefield: some observations on the theory, practice and politics of feminist literary criticism', *Feminist Studies*, 6 (Summer 1980), 1–25. See Jane Marcus, 'Storming the toolshed', *Signs*, 7 (Spring 1982), 622–25 and Judith Gardner *et al*. 'An interchange on feminist criticism: On 'Dancing through the minefield', *Feminist Studies*, 8 (Autumn 1982), 629–75 for a variety of objections to Kolodny.
30. Cited by Marcus, 'Storming the toolshed', 623 n.3.
31. Marxist Feminist Literature Collective, 'Women's Writing', 27.
32. Women's time', 35.

Chapter Two The Canon

1. Virago Press has done a great deal to bring women writers back into print in Britain, and many of their volumes are now available in the US through Penguin. *The Young Rebecca*, edited for Virago by Jane Marcus, introduces West's feminist and socialist essays and journalism. West's *Harriet Hume*, also published by Virago deserves attention as a modernist text. Articles on H.D. are cited in chapter 4.

2. *The Egoist*, December 1919, 71.
3. See Shari Benstock, *Women of the Left Bank* and Noel Riley Fitch, *Sylvia Beach and the Lost Generation*. I discuss Joyce's female publishing contexts more extensively in *Joyce and Feminism*, 85–115.
4. *The Very Rich Hours of Adrienne Monnier*, ed Richard McDougall, 71.
5. 'The power to name: some reflections on the avant garde', in *The Prism of Sex: Essays in the Sociology of Knowledge*, ed Julia A. Sherman and Evelyn Torton Beck, 55–77.
6. For a summary of woman's place in the institutional matrix of cheap popular fiction of the era, see Janice Radway, *Reading the Romance: Women, Patriarchy, and Popular Literature*, 19–27. Female readers of romances today prefer a fiesty heroine according to Radway—a preference they share with the boy an 'An Encounter'.
7. *James Joyce's Ulysses*, 30.
8. 'Nestor', in *James Joyce's Ulysses: Critical Essays*, ed Clive Hart and David Hayman, 22.
9. Ruth Bauerle suggests that Joyce's mother was the victim of marital rape, 'Date rape/mate rape', *New Alliances in Joyce Studies*, ed Bonnie Kime Scott.
10. The myth of Daphne encourages us to consider the tree a safe transformation for a female figure. Scholars have found this same riddle in Swift's *Polite Conversation*, a work written with an anticipated female audience and featuring female society, though one which also trivializes women.
11. The famous fantasy of Shakespeare's sister is in *A Room of One's Own*, 48–50.
12. See Nancy K. Miller, *The Heroine's Text*, x–xi.
13. The critical identification of the word known to all men had been omitted from previous editions of *Ulysses* and became readily available to readers with the publication of its Critical and Synoptic Edition in 1984.
14. *A Room of One's Own*, 68.
15. My list of major figures alluded to is derived from James Atherton's essay, 'The Oxen of the Sun', in the much-used collection, Clive Hart and David Hayman (eds), *James Joyce's Ulysses*, 313–39.
16. At the 1985 Joyce Conference in Philadelphia, Senn convened daily workshop sessions on 'Oxen'; more sporadic workshops began in the late 1970s.
17. Sandra M. Gilbert and Susan Gubar, 'Sexual linguistics', *New Literary History*, 16.3 (1985), 534: 'The so-called "Oxen of the Sun" chapter, after all, records the conception, incubation, and birth— "Hoopsa Boyaboy Hoopsa"—of a magical-sounding boy through a series of stylistic metamorphoses which seem to prove that (male) linguistic ontogeny recapitulates (male) linguistic phylogeny.' My experience with women readers of the chapter is that they always

want to discuss the marginalization of Mina Purefoy and the actual birth experience.

18. Carolyn Heilbrun, *Reinventing Womanhood*, 114–5.
19. Joyce, like Stephen, had offered an unfavourable review of Gregory (*CW*, 102–5). His broadside, 'The Holy Office' makes fun of Yeats' appeasement of 'his giddy dames' frivolities' (*CW* 150).
20. *Third Census of Finnegans Wake*, 179. 'If Mackay [Corelli's actual name] is comprehended in Maggies ... , then the Maggies are purveyors of female fiction which prettifies and sexifies "the colours of good and evil" that are "The Mime".'
21. 'Modern fiction', in *The Common Reader*, 154–7.
22. One interesting moment of female history preserved in the *Wake* is the Married Women's Property Act (*FW* 617. 34–5). John Stuart Mill's *The Subjection of Women* is also alluded to (213.2).
23. Bernard Benstock has detected Florence Nightingale in this section of the *Wake*. See *Joyce-Again's Wake*, 171–2.

Chapter Three Gender, discourse and culture

1. *The Archaeology of Knowledge and The Discourse on Language*, trans. A. M. Sheridan Smith, 117.
2. Colin MacCabe suggests that the father's authority as narrator is juxtaposed by the sound of the mother in this opening scene. See *James Joyce and the Revolution of the Word*, 55–6. I work more on this aspect as maternal semiotics in chapter 5.
3. *Joyce's Voices*, 39, 45.
4. 'Castration or decapitation?', *Signs*, 7.1 (1981), 54.
5. 'Disremembering Dedalus: *A Portrait of the Artist as a Young Man*', in *Untying the Text: A Post-Structuralist Reader*, ed Robert Young, 202–3.
6. Roberta M. Hall, 'The classroom climate: a chilly one for women?', 8–9
7. *The Book as World*, 145–8.
8. 'Gerty MacDowell: Joyce's sentimental heroine', in *Women in Joyce* ed Suzette Henke and Elaine Unkeless, 82–107.
9. Sandra M. Gilbert and Susan Gubar, 'Sexual linguistics: gender, language, sexuality', *New Literary History*, 16.3 (1985), 515–43.
10. *Writing beyond the Ending: Narrative Strategies of Twentieth-Century Women Writers*
11. *Reading the Romance: Women, Patriarchy, and Popular Literature*, 3–5, 119–156.
12. Radway, *Reading the Romance*, 131–2. Radway has found that present-day readers of pulp romances dislike texts that feature sexual details, making them comparable to Gerty (67).
13. *The Heroine's Text*, xi.

14. Richard Brown discusses the vogue for works on adultery in *James Joyce and Sexuality*, 16–22.
15. The 1984 edition restores Stephen's thoughts in Latin along these lines to the 'Scylla and Charybdis' episode: 'Love, yes. Word known to all men. *Amor vero aliquid alicui bonum vult unde et ea quae concupiscimus.*' He is summarizing Aquinas' *Summa contra Gentiles*.

Chapter Four Myths of female origins

1. T. S. Eliot, '*Ulysses*, order and myth', *Dial*, 75 (November 1923), 480–3. In *James Joyce: The Critical Heritage*, ed Robert Deming, 192–4. A. Walton Litz suggests that Eliot delayed his review of *Ulysses* out of ambivalence until he hit upon the classicist justification. See 'Pound and Eliot on *Ulysses*: the critical tradition', in *Ulysses: Fifty Years*, ed Thomas F. Staley, 16.
2. 'Sexual linguistics: gender, language, sexuality', *New Literary History* 16.3 (1985), 532–3.
3. Richard Ellmann, *The Consciousness of Joyce*, 39–44. Fritz Senn, 'Remodeling Homer', in *Light Rays: James Joyce and Modernism*, 70–92. Senn uses the phrase 'modeln times' (*FW* 289. n.6) to suggest that '*Finnegans Wake* is energy that modulates itself, that modulates times and reshapes words, by a man ... who had steadily been reshaping classical models' and whose works 'also modeled new types of readers' (71). It is of some interest that the phrase seized on by Senn is provided by a female figure, Issy.
4. For a feminist interpretation of the Lamb family, see Louise Bernikow, *Among Women*, 49–53.
5. Thomas Connolly, *The Personal Library of James Joyce: A Descriptive Bibliography*, 19.
6. Samuel Butler's theories of female authorship of *The Odyssey* are summarized by Richard Brown in his *James Joyce and Sexuality*, 102. See also Butler, *The Authoress of 'The Odyssey'*.
7. Elliott Gose, 'Joyce's goddess of generation', paper presented at the James Joyce Symposium, Dublin, June 1982.
8. Evelyn Haller celebrates the presence of Egyptian myth in Woolf, failing to acknowledge its presence in *Finnegans Wake*. Haller, 'Isis Unveiled: Virginia Woolf's use of Egyptian Myth', in *Virginia Woolf: A Feminist Slant*, ed Jane Marcus, 113. For a corrective, see Suzette Henke, 'James Joyce East and Middle-East: literary resonances of Judaism, Egyptology, and Indian Myth'.
9. 'Sexual linguistics', 534.
10. William Herman, 'Virginia Woolf and the Classics: every Englishman's prerogative transmuted into fictional art', in *Virginia Woolf: Centennial Essays*, ed Elaine K. Ginsberg and Laura Moss Gottlieb, 267.

11. Philip E. Slater, *The Glory of Hera*, 3–74 and *passim*. An account of Greek family life is derived from court testimonies in W. K. Lacey's *The Family in Classical Greece*. While Lacey's interpretation does not emphasize misogyny, it does insist on the severe limitations placed on women in patriarchal Greek society. It offers better accounts of sex-role variations in different Greek eras, classes and locales.

12. Estella Lauter, *Women as Mythmakers*. I also recommend Annis Pratt, *Archetypal Patterns of Women's Fiction*. See also John B. Vickery, *The Literary Impact of The Golden Bough*, who considers these three writers and Joyce.

13. *The Years*, 104–6.

14. Rachel Blau DuPlessis, *Writing beyond the Ending: Narrative Strategies of Twentieth-Century Women Writers*, 81.

15. DuPlessis, 66–71. Joyce did little censoring, but apparently also little reading of modernist women writers. H.D.'s *Bid Me to Live* (61–2) repeatedly notes Lawrence's disapproval (as the character Rico) of the woman artist's writing as the male, Orpheus.

16. 'Circe/Mud Poems', in *You are Happy*, 47.

17. Lauter, *Women as Mythmakers*, 62–78.

18. DuPlessis, *Writing Beyond the Ending*, 110–2.

19. 'Hérétique de l'amour', *Tel Quel* 74 (Winter 1977). Summarized by Susan Rubin Suleiman, 'Writing and motherhood', in *The (M)other Tongue: Essays in Feminist Psychoanalytic Interpretation*, ed Shirley Nelson Garner, Claire Kahane and Madelon Sprengnether, 368–9.

20. 'Castration or decapitation?', trans. Annette Kuhn, *Signs* 7.1 (1981), 50–4.

21. Lauter, *Women as Mythmakers*, 212–19.

22. DuPlessis, *Writing Beyond the Ending*, 162–5.

23. Michel Foucault, *The History of Sexuality: Volume I: An Introduction*, trans. Robert Hurley, 154.

24. 'Castration or decapitation?' 46, 54.

25. 'Love, guilt and reparation', in *Love, Guilt and Reparation and other Works, 1921–1945*, 334. Cited by Suleiman, 'Writing and motherhood', 357.

26. Suleiman, 354.

27. 'Women's time', trans. Alice Jardine and Harry Blake, *Signs*, 7.1 (1981), 32.

28. Cixous, 'Castration or decapitation?', 45–6; Gilbert and Gubar, 'Sexual linguistics', 518.

29. Hélène Cixous, 'Joyce: the (r)use of writing', in *Post-structuralist Joyce*, ed Derek Attridge and Daniel Ferrer, 15–17.29.

30. I recommend Edmund Epstein, *The Ordeal of Stephen Dedalus* and Sheldon Brivic, *Joyce between Freud and Jung*.

31. Florence Howe, 'Feminism and literature', in *Images of Women in Fiction: Feminist Perspectives*, ed Susan Koppelman Cornillon, 260.

32. See Slater, *The Glory of Hera*, 77.
33. Zack Bowen identifies the reference to prostitution as a song in Head's *Canting Academy*. *Musical Allusions in the Works of James Joyce*, 79.
34. The chapter also offers an additional encounter of his father as Dedalus, when Simon swoops in, also fulfilling the patriarchal device of the Joyce coat of arms (*U* 15.3944ff). The Dedalus father figure receives its final dismissal here, in the company of Mr Deasy, as Stephen takes up his ritual dance with Zoe. Both Dedalus and the devouring mother are concepts Stephen must dispatch from his unconscious.
35. Stuart Gilbert, *James Joyce's Ulysses*, 316–19, 334, 345. See Gilbert's note on the *Attis* poem of Catullus (LXIII) for interesting parallels concerning the ritual dances for the great mother, Cybele, Tellus, rites including frenzied excitement and self-castration on the part of male worshippers. These rituals are represented in *The Golden Bough*, though Joyce's reading of Frazer's accounts previous to the publication of *Ulysses* has not been established. Vickery compares Bella to 'orgiastic fertility goddesses whose dedication to unbridled lust is matched only by their readiness to put their lovers to death' (399). Vickery centres on Stephen as dying god and Bloom as scapegoat in a study of 'Circe' that has very little of a positive sort to say about its female figures (375–404).
36. On the theme of adultery in nineteenth-century literature, see Richard Brown, *James Joyce and Sexuality*, 19–28.
37. Daniel Ferrer, 'Circe, regret and regression', in *Post-structuralist Joyce*, ed Derek Attridge and Daniel Ferrer, 134–7.
38. Grace Eckley is an exception to this. She makes a good case for the 'Anna Livia' chapter's providing a basic dialogic structure for the work as a whole. Michael H. Begnal and Grace Eckley, *Narrator and Character in Finnegans Wake*, 130ff.
39. Margot Norris presents as the last of five themes of the *Wake*, 'Redemption: maternal salvage'. Her analysis valorizes ALP's collecting efforts. It places them mainly in a Christian, rather than a pre-Greek, pagan mythic structure. See *The Decentered Universe of Finnegans Wake*, 64–72.
40. For a beautiful translation and interpretation of Inanna's myths, see Diane Wolkstein and Samuel Noah Kramer, '*Inanna: Queen of Heaven and Earth: Her Stories and Hymns from Sumer*.
41. 'Anna Livia Plurabelle: the dream woman', in *Woman in Joyce* ed Suzette Henke and Elaine Unkeless, 209.
42. Diane Griffin Crowder, 'Amazons and mothers? Monique Wittig, Hélène Cixous and theories of women's writing', *Contemporary Literature*, 24.2 (1983), 122–4.
43. Nor Hall, *The Moon and the Virgin*, 189.
44. Cixous says of woman's place, 'She is outside the city, at the edge of the city—the city is man, ruled by masculine law. . . . ' 'Castration or decapitation?', 49.

45. For the sense of rape in the song, I am grateful to Ruth Bauerle, 'Date rape/mate rape: two contemporary issues in 'The Dead', in *New Alliances in Joyce Studies* ed Bonnie Kime Scott.

46. 'ALP: the dream woman', 199.

47. Nancy K. Miller notes that, even with twentieth-century women writers, the 'female *Bildung* tends to get stuck in the bedroom'. *The Heroine's Text*, 157. Cixous protests Joyce's tendency to put women into beds: Excursion of Penelope-Everywoman: sickbed in which the mother never gets done with dying, hospital bed in which Madame Purefoy never gets done with giving birth, bed of Molly the wife, the adulteress, setting of an infinite erotic reverie, excursion of reminiscences.' 'La jeune née', trans. Meg Bortin, *Diacritics* (June 1977), 66–7.

48. A paper by Joe Taylor in my 1984 graduate Joyce seminar has encouraged me to think of Molly as a wanderer comparable to Ulysses.

49. MS in the British Library.

50. Begnal and Eckley, *Narrator and Character*, 41.

51. 'Women's time', 13–35.

52. *ibid.*, 31

53. *ibid.*, 34.

54. Richard Brown, *James Joyce and Sexuality* offers a discussion of intermediate sexuality, a third sex, etc., offering examples from *Ulysses* and *Finnegans Wake*, 106–7.

55. Wyndham Lewis, *Satire and Fiction*,43.

56. Virginia Woolf, 'Modern fiction', in *The Common Reader*, 154.

57. Wyndham Lewis, *The Apes of God*, 78. The comparability is noted by the editor of the 1981 edition, Paul Edwards, 'Afterword', 636–7.

58. *Satire and Fiction*, 47.

59. Wyndham Lewis, *Blast*, 1 (June 1914), 23.

60. Kenner's *Wyndham Lewis*, remains a fine introduction to Lewis and his concept of 'vorticism'. Lewis is the subject of Jameson's *Fables of Aggression*. Kenner and Jameson would provide interesting material for future feminist analysis of the history of modernist criticism. Joyce is of course capable of assigning geometry to ALP, as Margaret Solomon has investigated in *The Eternal Geomater*, 105–6. I consider Solomon's book pre-feminist. It offers careful exegesis of the Prankquean's tale and the hen's letter and takes its title from the earth mother. Yet it concludes on HCE as father God and his cubic geometry.

Chapter Five Gender, language and writing

1. Clive Hart and Margot Norris both maintain this view, though Begnal and Eckley have proposed more voices. Hart, *Structure and Motif in Finnegans Wake*; Norris, *The Decentered Universe of Finnegans*

Wake; Michae H. Begnal and Grace Eckley, *Narrator and Character in Finnegans Wake*.

2. Sandra M. Gilbert and Susan Gubar, 'Sexual linguistics: gender, language, sexuality', *New Literary History*, 16.3 (1985), 532–5. Hugh Kenner's interpretation of tradition, Joyce and literary history, supports this sort of reading of Joyce. The novel, or 'easy book' began with the education of women, and was designed for people who had never read anything else. Kenner seems relieved that, with Joyce's inclusion of the parodic tradition in the novel, it has been brought to academic respectability. 'How on earth have we *ever* read Joyce', paper presented at the 8th International Joyce Symposium, Frankfurt, June 1984.

3. Begnal and Eckley, *Narrator and Character* 48.

4. For comparable syntactical-sexual word play, see Leopold Bloom's parsing of the sentence 'He fucked her' in active and passive cases in the scientific jargon parodied in the 'Ithaca' episode of *Ulysses* (*U* 17.2217–23).

5. 'Sexual linguistics', 530. *Palimpsest* (1926) is the title of a collection of fiction by H.D.

6. *Between the Acts*, 152–3.

7. *The Eternal Geomater*, 60–63, 77–78. The letter T is the phallus and the letter P is the vulva in Solomon's exegesis.

8. For a thorough discussion of the transforming styles of *Ulysses* and a definition of the 'initial style', see Karen Lawrence, *The Odyssey of Styles in Ulysses*.

9. 'Inlaws/outlaws: the language of women', in *Women's Language and Style*, ed. Douglas Butturff and Edmund L. Epstein, 2–3. The talk of Issy's twenty-eight girls often merely echoes socialized feminine norms, though in the ancient rituals resembling keening, they achieve more of a 'pollylogue' (*FW* 470.9).

10. For more discussion of Issy's use of language, see Shari Benstock, 'Nightletters: woman's writing in the *Wake*', in *Critical Essays on Joyce* ed Bernard Benstock, 221–33.

11. Robin Tolmach Lakoff's original work is in her *Language and Woman's Place*. In chapter 3, I dealt to some extent with Gerty MacDowell's use of language. See also my *Joyce and Feminism* for studies of the language of Emma Clery and Molly Bloom, 133–83.

12. As an introduction to *fémininité* and *l'écriture féminine*, see Ann Russell Jones, 'Writing the body: toward an understanding of *l'écriture féminine*', *Feminist Studies*, 7.2 (Summer 1981), 247–63.

13. *A Writer's Diary*, 349.

14. Nancy K. Miller, 'Emphasis added: plots and plausibilities in women's fiction', *PMLA*, 96.1 (1981), 40.

15. Maud Ellman works with language and lips, Stephen's as well as his mother's, in 'Disremembering Dedalus: *A Portrait of the Artist as a Young Man*', in *Untying the Text: A Post-Structuralist Reader*, ed Robert Young, 190.

16. Luce Irigaray, from 'This sex which is not one', in *New French Feminisms*, ed Elaine Marks and Isabelle de Courtivron (University of Massachusetts Press, Amherst, 1980), 100–1, 103.
17. Nancy Chodorow, *The Reproduction of Mothering*, 167.
18. Colin MacCabe identifies this scene as an example of 'a minimal pleasure to be taken in the mother-tongue'. *James Joyce and the Revolution of the Word*, 67.
19. Robin Tolmach Lakoff, 'Women's language', in *Women's Language and Style*, ed. Butturff and Epstein, 152.
20. Virginia Woolf, *A Room of One's Own*.
21. 'Sexual linguistics', 532–3.
22. Kristeva, 'The Father, love and banishment', in *Desire in Language: A Semiotic Approach to Literature and Art*, ed Leon Roudiez, 157.
23. Stuart Gilbert, *James Joyce's Ulysses*, 30. The list of organs, interestingly, includes the womb but not the penis. This might be expected to be the organ of 'Lotos eaters', but Joyce opts for an ungendered designation, 'genitals'. I can read this two ways: positively, as a de-emphasis of the penis, which in this chapter is limp anyhow, or negatively, as if the male's penis is the universal genital organ.
24. Clive Hart associates 'anastomosis' with intercourse. See *Structure and Motif in Finnegans Wake*, 154–60.
25. There seems to be a comparable message in the following: Lets have a fuchu all around, courting cousins! Quuck, the duck of a woman for quack, the drake of a man, her little live apples for Leas and love potients for Leos, the next beast king. ... I can see you sprouting scruples. Get back. And as he's boiling with water I'll light your pyre. Turn about, skeezy Sammy, out of metaphor, till we feel you still tropeful of popetry. (*FW* 466.4–11)
26. 'The laugh of Medusa', *Signs* (1976); reprinted in *New French Feminisms*, ed Elaine Marks and Isabelle de Courtivron, 260.
27. Irigaray, from 'This sex which is not one', in *New French Feminisms*, 103.
28. H. G. Wells coined the term in his review of *A Portrait*.
29. Solomon, *The Eternal Geomater*, 60, 90.
30. 'Writing and motherhood', in *The (M)other Tongue: Essays in Feminist Psychoanalytic Interpretation*, ed Shirley Nelson Gardner, Claire Kahane, and Madelon Sprengnether, 356–60.
31. 'Nightletters', 230. Though this satisfies a Derridean paradigm of dissemination on the hymen, I find the hymen unlikely stationery for the sexually-experienced ALP. Derrida retains the penis as writing instrument, while the hen has her own beak.
32. 'Teaching *Finnegans Wake* from a feminist perspective', unpublished paper presented at SUNY, Purchase, February 1982.
33. 'The blank page' and issues of female creativity', *Critical Inquiry* 8.2 (1981), 243–63. Shirley Peterson, my student in a 1984 Joyce graduate seminar, drew my attention to the applicability of this essay to

Molly. Susan Gubar, 'Blessings in disguise: cross-dressing as re-dressing for female modernists'. *Massachusetts Review*, 22 (Autumn 1981), 478; 477–508 *passim*.

34. For more on alphabets, see Grace Eckley, *Narrator and Character in Finnegans Wake*, 148–52.

35. If this were a chapter on sex roles instead of language, we might look at Martha as part of the phenomenon of women and technology.

36. Bernard Benstock offers a more male-centred interpretation and critical language in considering the final 'the': That both *Diu* and *The* have a missing letter suggests the lost phallus of the emasculated god.... The *Wake* significantly ends with the word 'the', ... a modulation from the strongest word in any language, the word for God, to the emasculated form which Joyce considered the weakest word in the English language. *Joyce–Again's Wake*, 113n.

Bibliography

Atherton, James, 'The oxen of the sun', in Clive Hart and David Hayman (eds), *James Joyce's Ulysses: Critical Essays*, 313–39.

Attridge, Derek and Ferrer, Daniel (eds), *Post-Structuralist Joyce: From the French* (Cambridge University Press, Cambridge, 1984).

Atwood, Margaret, 'Circe/Mud Poems' in *You are Happy* (Harper & Row, New York, 1974), 45–70.

Auerbach, Nina. *Woman and the Demon: the Life of a Victorian Myth*. (Harvard University Press, Cambridge, 1982).

Bauerle, Ruth, 'Date rape/mate rape: two contemporary issues in "The Dead"', in Bonnie Scott (ed) *New Alliances in Joyce Studies*.

Begnal, Michael H. and Eckley, Grace, *Narrator and Character in Finnegans Wake* (Bucknell University Press, Lewisburg, 1975).

Benstock, Bernard, *Joyce-Again's Wake* (University of Washington Press, Seattle and London, 1965).

—— (ed), *Critical Essays on Joyce* (G.K. Hall & Co., Boston, 1985).

Benstock, Shari, 'Nightletters: woman's writing in the *Wake*', in Bernard Benstock (ed), *Critical Essays on Joyce*, 221–33.

——, *Women of the Left Bank* (University of Texas Press, Austin, 1986.

Bernikow, Louise, *Among Women* (Harper & Row, New York, 1980).

Bowen, Zack, *Musical Allusions in the Works of James Joyce* (SUNY Press, Albany, 1974).

Brivic, Sheldon, *Joyce between Freud and Jung* (Kennikat, Port Washington, NY, 1980).

Brown, Richard, *James Joyce and Sexuality* (Cambridge University Press, Cambridge, 1985).

Butler, Samuel, *The Authoress of 'The Odyssey'* (Fifield, London, 1895).

Butturff, Douglas and Epstein, Edmund L. (eds), *Women's Language and Style* (L & S Books, Akron, 1978).

142

Culler, Jonathan, *On Deconstruction: Theory and Criticism after Structuralism* (Cornell University Press, Ithaca, 1982).

Chodorow, Nancy, *The Reproduction of Mothering* (University of California Press, Berkeley, 1978).

Cixous, Hélène, 'The laugh of Medusa', trans. Keith Cohen and Park Cohen, *Signs*, 1.4 (Summer 1976), 875–893. Reprinted in Elaine Marks and Isabelle de Courtivron (eds), *New French Feminisms: An Anthology*.

—— 'La jeune née', trans. Meg Bortin, *Diacritics*, 7.2 (Summer 1977), 64–69.

——, 'Castration or decapitation?', trans. Annette Kuhn, *Signs*, 7.1 (Autumn 1981), 41–55.

——, 'Joyce: the (r)use of writing', in Derek Attridge and Daniel Ferrer (eds), *Post-Structuralist Joyce*, 15–30.

Connolly, Thomas, *The Personal Library of James Joyce: A Descriptive Bibliography* (University of Buffalo, Buffalo, 1955).

Cornillon, Susan Koppelman (ed), *Images of Women in Fiction: Feminist Perspectives* (Bowling Green University Popular Press, Bowling Green, Ohio, 1972).

Crowder, Diane Griffin, 'Amazons and mothers? Monique Wittig, Hélène Cixous and theories of women's writing', *Contemporary Literature*, 24.2 (1983), 117–44.

De Beauvoir, Simone, *The Second Sex* (Knopf, New York, 1953).

Deming, Robert (ed), *James Joyce: The Critical Heritage* (Routledge & Kegan Paul, London, 1970).

DuPlessis, Rachel Blau, *Writing beyond the Ending: Narrative Strategies of Twentieth-Century Women Writers* (Indiana University Press, Bloomington, 1985).

Duyfhuizen, Bernard, 'Deconstruction and feminist literary theory', *Tulsa Studies in Women's Literature*, 3.1/2 (1984), 159–67.

Edwards, Paul, 'Afterword' to Wyndham Lewis, *The Apes of God* (Black Sparrow Press, Santa Barbara, 1981), 629–39.

Ehrlich, Heyward (ed), *Light Rays: James Joyce and Modernism* (New Horizon Press, New York, 1984).

Eliot, T.S., '*Ulysses*, order and myth', *Dial*, 75 (November 1923), 480–3. Reprinted in Robert Deming (ed), *James Joyce: The Critical Heritage*.

Ellmann, Mary, *Thinking about Women* (Harcourt, Brace, Jovanovich, New York, 1968).

Ellmann, Maud, 'Disremembering Dedalus: *A Portrait of the Artist as a Young Man*', in Robert Young (ed), *Untying the Text: A Post-Structuralist Reader*, 189–206.

Ellmann, Richard, *The Consciousness of Joyce* (Oxford University Press, Toronto and New York, 1977).

Epstein, Edmund, *The Ordeal of Stephen Dedalus* (Southern Illinois University Press, Carbondale, 1971).

——, 'Nestor', in Clive Hart and David Hayman (eds), *James Joyce's Ulysses: Critical Essays*, 17–28.

Ferrer, Daniel, 'Circe, regret and regression', in Derek Attridge and Daniel Ferrer (eds), *Post-Structuralist Joyce*, 127–144.

Fitch, Noel Riley, *Sylvia Beach and the Lost Generation* (Norton, New York, 1983, and Souvenir Press, London, 1984).

Foucault, Michael, *The Archaeology of Knowledge and The Discourse on Language*, trans. A.M. Sheridan Smith (Pantheon Books, New York, 1972).

——, *The History of Sexuality: Volume I: An Introduction*, trans. Robert Hurley (Pantheon Books, New York, 1978).

Frazer, James, *The Golden Bough*. A New Abridgment, ed Theodore H. Gaster (New American Library, New York, 1959).

French, Marilyn, *The Book as World* (Harvard University Press, Cambridge, Mass., 1975).

Friedman, Susan Stanford, *Psyche Reborn* (Indiana University Press, Bloomington, 1981).

Gallop, Jane, *Feminism and Psychoanalysis: The Daughter's Seduction* (Macmillan, London, 1982).

Gardner, Judith Kegan, Balkin, Elly, Patterson, Rena Grasso and Kolodny, Annette, 'An interchange on feminist criticism: on "Dancing through the minefield"', *Feminist Studies*, 8.3 (Fall 1982), 629–75.

Garner, Shirley Nelson, Kahane, Claire and Sprengnether, Madelon (eds), *The (M)other Tongue: Essays in Feminist Psychoanalytic Interpretation* (Cornell University Press, Ithaca and London, 1985).

Gilbert, Sandra M. and Gubar, Susan, *The Madwoman in the Attic* (Yale University Press, New Haven, 1979).

——, 'Sexual linguistics: gender, language, sexuality', *New Literary History*, 16.3 (1985), 515–543.

Gilbert, Stuart, *James Joyce's Ulysses* (Vintage, New York, 1952).

Ginsberg, Elaine K. and Gottlieb, Laura Moss (eds), *Virginia Woolf: Centennial Essays* (Whiston, Troy, New York, 1983).

Glasheen, Adaline, *Third Census of Finnegans Wake* (University of California Press, Berkeley, 1977).

Gose, Elliott, 'Joyce's goddess of generation', paper presented at the James Joyce Symposium, Dublin, June 1982.

Griffin, Susan, *Woman and Nature: The Roaring Inside Her* (Harper & Row, New York, 1980).

——, 'The way of all ideology', *Signs*, 7.3 (Spring 1982), 641–60.

Gubar, Susan, '"The blank page" and issues of female creativity', *Critical Inquiry*, 8.2 (1981), 243–63.

——, 'Blessings in disguise: cross-dressing as re-dressing for female modernists', *Massachusetts Review*, 22.4 (1981), 477–508.

Hall, Nor, *The Moon and the Virgin* (Harper & Row, New York, 1980).

Hall, Roberta M., 'The classroom climate: a chilly one for women?' (Project on the Status and Education of Women, Association of American Colleges, 1982).

Haller, Evelyn, 'Isis unveiled: Virginia Woolf's use of Egyptian myth', in Jane Marcus (ed), *Virginia Woolf: A Feminist Slant*, 109–31.

Hart, Clive, *Structure and Motif in Finnegans Wake* (Northwestern University Press, Evanston, IL., 1962).

Hart, Clive and Hayman, David (eds), *James Joyce's Ulysses: Critical Essays* (University of California Press, Berkeley, 1974).

H.D., *Bid Me to Live* (Dial Press, New York, 1960).

——, *Palimpsest*. (1926; Southern Illinois University Press, Carbondale, 1968).

Heilbrun, Carolyn, *Reinventing Womanhood* (W.W. Norton, New York, 1979).

Henke, Suzette, 'Gerty MacDowell: Joyce's sentimental heroine', in Suzette Henke and Elaine Unkeless (eds), *Women in Joyce*, 132–49.

——, 'Stephen Dedalus and Women: a portrait of the artist as a young misogynist', in Suzette Henke and Elaine Unkeless (eds), *Women in Joyce*, 82–107.

——, 'James Joyce east and middle east: literary resonances of Judaism, Egyptology, and Indian myth, *The Journal of Modern Literature*, forthcoming.

Henke, Suzette and Unkeless, Elaine (eds), *Women in Joyce* (University of Illinois Press, Urbana, 1982).

Herman, William, 'Virginia Woolf and the Classics; every Englishman's prerogative transmuted into fictional art', in Elaine K. Ginsberg and Laura Moss Gottlieb (eds), *Virginia Woolf: Centennial Essays*, 257–68.

Howe, Florence, 'Feminism and literature', in Susan Koppelman Cornillon (ed), *Images of Women in Fiction: Feminist Perspectives*, 253–77.

Irigaray, Luce, *Speculum de l'autre femme* (Editions de Minuit, Paris, 1974).

——, 'This sex which is not one', in Elaine Marks and Isabelle de Courtivron (eds), *New French Feminisms: An Anthology*. Originally published as '*Ce sexe qui n'en est pas un* (Editions de Minuit, Paris, 1977).

Jameson, Frederic, *Fables of Aggression* (University of California Press, Berkeley, 1979).

Jardine, Alice, 'Gynesis', *Diacritics*, 7/8 (1978), 54–65.

Johnston, Judith, "Teaching *Finnegans Wake* from a feminist perspective', unpublished paper presented at SUNY, Purchase, February 1982.

Jones, Ann Russell, 'Writing the body: toward an understanding of l'écriture féminine', *Feminist Studies*, 7.2 (Summer 1981), 247–63.

Kenner, Hugh, *Wyndham Lewis* (New Directions, Norfolk, CT, 1954).

——, *Joyce's Voices* (University of California Press, Berkeley, 1978).

——, 'How on earth have we *ever* read Joyce?' unpublished paper presented at 8th International Joyce Symposium, Frankfurt, June 1984.

Klein, Melanie, *Love, Guilt and Reparation and Other Works, 1921–1945* (1937; Doubleday, New York, 1977).

Kolodny, Annette, 'A map for rereading: or, gender and the interpretation of literary texts', *New Literary History*, 2 (Spring 1980), 451–67, rpt. Elaine Showalter (ed), *The New Feminist Criticism*.

——, 'Dancing through the minefield; some observations on the theory, practice and politics of feminist literary criticism', *Feminist Studies*, 6 (Summer 1980), 1–25.

Kristeva, Julia, 'Hérétique de l'amour', *Tel Quel*, 74 (Winter 1977).

——, 'The father, love and banishment', in Leon Roudiez (ed), *Desire in Language: A Semiotic Approach to Literature and Art*, 148–58.

——, 'Women's time', trans. Alice Jardine and Harry Blake, *Signs*, 7.1 (Autumn 1981), 13–35.

Lacey, W.K., *The Family in Classical Greece* (Cornell University Press, Ithaca, 1968).

Lakoff, Robin Tolmach, *Language and Woman's Place* (Harper & Row, New York, 1975).

—— , 'Women's language', in Douglas Butturff and Edmund L. Epstein (eds), *Women's Language and Style*, 139–58.

Lauter, Estella, *Women as Mythmakers* (Indiana University

Press, Bloomington, 1984).

Lawrence, D.H., *Women in Love* (1920; Viking Press, New York, 1968).

Lawrence, Karen, *The Odyssey of Styles in Ulysses* (Princeton University Press, Princeton, 1981).

Lerner, Gerda, *The Majority Finds its Past* (Oxford University Press, New York, 1979).

Lewis, Wyndham, 'The great preliminary vortex: manifesto–I', *Blast*, 1 (June 1914), 11–29.

——, *Satire and Fiction* (Arthur Press, London, 1930).

——, *The Apes of God* (1930; Black Sparrow Press, Santa Barbara, 1981).

Litz, A. Walton, 'Pound and Eliot on *Ulysses*: the critical tradition', in Thomas F. Staley (ed), *Ulysses: Fifty Years*.

MacCabe, Colin, *James Joyce and the Revolution of the Word* (Macmillan, London, 1979).

McDougall, Richard (ed), *The Very Rich Hours of Adrienne Monnier* (Scribner's, New York, 1976).

Makward, Christiane, 'Interview with Hélène Cixous', trans. Ann Liddle and Beatrice Cameron, *Sub Stance*, 13 (1976).

Marcus, Jane, 'Storming the toolshed', *Signs*, 7.3 (Spring 1982), 622–40.

—— (ed), *Virginia Woolf: A Feminist Slant* (University of Nebraska Press, Lincoln, 1983).

—— (ed), *The Young Rebecca*, by Rebecca West (Virago, London, 1983).

——, 'Still practice, a w/rested alphabet: toward a feminist aesthetic', *Tulsa Studies in Women's Literature*, 3.1/2 (1984).

Marks, Elaine, 'Woman and literature in France', *Signs*, 3.4 (Summer 1978), 832–42.

Marks, Elaine and Isabelle de Courtivron (eds), *New French Feminisms: An Anthology* (University of Massachusetts Press, Amherst and Harvester Press, Brighton, 1980).

Marxist-Feminist Literature Collective, 'Women's writing: Jane Eyre, Shirley, Villette, Aurora Leigh', *Ideology and Consciousness*, 3 (Spring 1978), 27–48.

Miller, Nancy K., *The Heroine's Text* (Columbia University Press, New York, 1980).

——, 'Emphasis added: plots and plausibilities in women's fiction', *PMLA*, 96.1 (1981), 36–48.

Mitchell, Juliet and Rose, Jacqueline (eds), *Feminine Sexuality: Jacques Lacan and the École Freudienne* (Macmillan, London, 1982).

Moi, Toril, *Sexual/Textual Politics: Feminist Literary Theory*, (London and New York: Methuen, 1985).

Monnier, Adrienne, *The Very Rich Hours of Adrienne Monnier*, ed Richard McDougall (Scribners, New York, 1976).

Norris, Margot, *The Decentered Universe of Finnegans Wake* (The Johns Hopkins University Press, Baltimore and London, 1974).

——, 'Anna Livia Plurabelle: the dream woman', in Suzette Henke and Elaine Unkeless (eds) *Women in Joyce*, 197–213.

Pratt, Annis, *Archetypal Patterns of Women's Fiction* (Indiana University Press, Bloomington, 1981).

Radway, Janice, *Reading the Romance: Women, Patriarchy, and Popular Literature* (University of North Carolina Press, Chapel Hill and London, 1984).

Roudiez, Leon S. (ed), *Desire in Language: A Semiotic Approach to Literature*, by Julia Kristeva (Columbia University Press, New York, 1980).

Scott, Bonnie Kime, *Joyce and Feminism*, Indiana University Press, Bloomington and Harvester Press, Brighton, 1984).

—— (ed), *New Alliances in Joyce Studies* (University of Delaware Press, Newark, DE) forthcoming.

Senn, Fritz, 'Remodeling Homer', in Heyward Ehrlich (ed), *Light Rays: James Joyce and Modernism*, 70–92.

Sherman, Julia A. and Beck, Evelyn Torton (eds), *The Prism of Sex: Essays in the Sociology of Knowledge* (University of Wisconsin Press, Madison, 1979).

Showalter, Elaine, *A Literature of their Own* (Princeton University Press, Princeton, 1977).

—— , 'Feminist criticism in the wilderness', *Critical Inquiry*, 8.2 (Winter 1981), 179–205; rpt. Elaine Showalter (ed), *The New Feminist Criticism*.

——, 'The future of feminist criticism', in *Feminist Literary Criticism* (National Humanities Center, Research Triangle Park, 1981), 65–89.

—— (ed), 'Women's time, women's space: writing the history of feminist criticism', *Tulsa Studies in Women's Literature*, 3.1/2 (1984), 29–43.

—— (ed), *The New Feminist Criticism: Essays on Women, Literature and Theory* (Pantheon Books, New York, 1985).

Slater, Philip E., *The Glory of Hera* (Beacon Press, Boston, 1968).

Solomon, Margaret, *The Eternal Geomater* (Southern Illinois University Press, Carbondale, and Feffer & Simons, London, 1969).

Spanier, Bonnie, Bloom, Alexander and Boroviak, Darlene (eds),

Toward a Balanced Curriculum (Schenkman, Cambridge, MA., 1984).

Spivak, Gayatri, 'Feminism and critical theory', *Women's Studies International Quarterly*, 1.3 (1978), 241–6.

Staley, Thomas F. (ed), *Ulysses: Fifty Years* (Indiana University Press, Bloomington and London, 1974).

Stimpson, Catharine, 'The mind, the body, and Gertrude Stein', *Critical Inquiry*, 3 (Spring 1977), 489–506.

———, 'The power to name: some reflections on the avant-garde', in Julia A. Sherman and Evelyn Torton Beck (eds), *The Prism of Sex: Essays in the Sociology of Knowledge*, 55–77.

Suleiman, Susan Rubin, 'Writing and motherhood', in Shirley Nelson Garner, Claire Kahane and Madelon Sprengnether (eds), *The (M)other Tongue: Essays in Feminist Psychoanalytic Interpretation*, 352–77.

Tiger, Virginia and Luria, Gina, 'Inlaws/outlaws: the language of women', in Douglas Butturff and Edmund L. Epstein (eds), *Women's Language and Style*, 1–10.

Vickery, John B., *The Literary Impact of the Golden Bough* (Princeton University Press, Princeton, 1973).

West, Rebecca, *Harriet Hume* (1929; Virago, London, 1980).

Wolkstein, Diane and Kramer, Samuel Noah, *Inanna: Queen of Heaven and Earth: Her Stories and Hymns from Sumer* (Harper & Row, New York, 1983).

Woolf, Virginia, *Jacob's Room* (1922; Harcourt Brace Jovanovich, San Diego, 1978).

———, 'Modern fiction', in *The Common Reader*, 1st series (1925; Harcourt Brace & World, New York, 1953), 150–58.

———, *Mrs. Dalloway* (1925; Harcourt Brace & World, 1953).

———, *A Room of One's Own* (1928; Harcourt Brace & World, New York, 1963).

———, *Orlando* (1928; Harcourt Brace Jovanovich, New York, 1956).

———, *The Years* (1937; Harcourt Brace Jovanovich, New York, 1969).

———, *Three Guineas* (1938; Harcourt Brace Jovanovich, New York, 1969).

———, *Between the Acts* (1941; Harcourt Brace Jovanovich, New York 1970).

———, *A Writer's Diary* (Harcourt Brace Jovanovich, New York, 1954).

Young, Robert (ed), *Untying the Text: A Post-Structuralist Reader* (Routledge & Kegan Paul, Boston, 1981).

Index